Welcome to Anglican Spiritual Traditions

Vicki K. Black

Morehouse Publishing
NEW YORK · HARRISBURG · DENVER

Unless otherwise noted, the Scripture quotations contained herein are from the New Revised Standard Version Bible, copyright © 1989 by the Division of Christian Education of the National Council of Churches of Christ in the U.S.A. Used by permission. All rights reserved.

Morehouse Publishing, 4775 Linglestown Road, Harrisburg, PA 17112

Morehouse Publishing, 445 Fifth Avenue, New York, NY 10016

Morehouse Publishing is an imprint of Church Publishing Incorporated. www.churchpublishing.org

Library of Congress Cataloging-in-Publication Data
Black, Vicki K.
  Welcome to Anglican spiritual traditions / Vicki K. Black.
     p. cm.
  Includes bibliographical references.
  ISBN 978-0-8192-2368-5 (pbk.) -- ISBN 978-0-8192-2722-5 (ebook)
1. Anglican Communion. 2. Spiritual life--Anglican Communion. 3. Christian life--Anglican authors. I. Title.
  BX5005.B53 2010
  248.4'83--dc22
                                        2010044760

Printed in the United States of America

in thanksgiving
for the Benedictine Group
at St. Andrew's Episcopal Church, Newcastle, Maine

Contents

Introduction

Markers along the Way

I have discovered that the very essence of spiritual formation is that it involves encounter and engagement with something/ Someone of whom I am profoundly ignorant. It seems right that initially I test the path I wish to consider for its reasonableness and its compassion. But it is equally appropriate for me to realize that there are times in which my present worldview is totally inadequate for me to receive the response I seek. So I must simply continue to give myself to that which I do not understand. In such a journey, how very much I value the guides of tradition and authority that give me occasional markers, letting me know that others have trod here before me.[1]

When I set out to write this volume of the *Welcome to . . .* series on church history and spiritual traditions, I had envisioned a book that focused on events and dates, people and ideas, that told some of the stories of how people living in the last two millennia have lived out their faith in the God they knew in Christ. But as I mulled over how so many stories could be told in an introduction as brief as this one must be, I came across a book on leadership that held up the Baptismal Covenant in the 1979 Book of Common Prayer as the foundation of all Christian ministry and leadership. I began to wonder if this was true. If so, how many of us in the church today really know our baptismal vows to be the basis and formative expression of our faith? What would the baptismal vows we affirm and reaffirm in our liturgies really look like enfleshed in the ordinary, day-to-day lives most of us live? How do the promises we speak inform and shape the decisions we make, the actions we take?

My work of compiling readings for the Speaking to the Soul page of the Episcopal Café (*www.episcopalcafe.org*) with its task of investigating the lives and writings of the people identified as holy in the church calendar has reminded me that there are deep and decided differences in the ways Christians have lived out their faith through the generations. The feast day of the nineteenth-century Anglo-Catholic priest James DeKoven, whose election as bishop was denied by a church deeply divided over ritual, is followed the next day by the commemoration of Gregory the Illuminator, the fourth-century bishop of the church in Armenia who, we are told, survived a dozen years of imprisonment in a bottomless pit, one of the more inventive and harrowing punishments devised by a fractured church and society. Hildegard of Bingen falls between the fifth-century Ninian of Galloway and the nineteenth-century Tractarian Edward Pusey. The Christian family is full of characters, some more appealing and compelling than others. The stories of their lives make for fascinating reading.

The common thread among all those distinctively different stories, I realized, was baptism. We each contribute to the weaving of a complex and intricate pattern of human life and faith that grows with each passing generation, but it is baptism that makes us one. In baptism we are united in Christ, according to our baptismal liturgy:

> There is one Body and one Spirit;
> There is one hope in God's call to us;
> One Lord, one Faith, one Baptism;
> One God and Father of all. (BCP 299)

That unity is a bold claim for a church that for two thousand years has been marked by dissension and strife, division and persecution within and without. How Christians have attempted to live out this "one Faith" is a story with multiple beginnings and endings, intricate plot lines and intriguing characters. And yet the early church spoke of this task of living the Christian life as one of being on the "way of life," as opposed to the "way of death": "There are two ways, one of life and one of death, but a great difference between the two ways. The way of life, then, is this: First, you shall love God who made you; second, love your neighbor as yourself, and do not do to another what you would not want done to you."[2]

CHRISTIANITY AS A WAY OF LIFE

In his recent book *Finding Our Way Again,* emergent theologian Brian McLaren tells the story of an interview he conducted with the social scientist Peter Senge. Visiting a local bookstore, Senge related, he had asked the manager what the most popular books were at the time. The most popular books, he learned, were those that gave advice on "how to get rich in the new information economy"; the second were "books about spirituality, and in particular, books about Buddhism." Dr. Senge, who practices Zen meditation himself, reflected on why books on Buddhism are so popular today. "I think it's because Buddhism presents itself as a way of life," he told McLaren, "and Christianity presents itself as a system of belief. So I would want to get Christian ministers thinking about how to rediscover their own faith as a way of life, because that's what people are searching for today. That's what they need most."[3]

It is this search for meaning in a world that has seemingly lost its way that brings many people to the church today. As we face the "new challenges of a new age," in a world defined by what it was and is no longer—"postmodern, postcolonial, post-Enlightenment, post-Christendom, post-Holocaust, post-9/11"[4]—many of us find ourselves moving through a "dark night" in which all our beliefs and images of God are called into question or no longer make sense. We are in need of spiritual traditions that not only talk *about* God, but are themselves a path to encountering that Mystery. We need a faith that is alive and supple, able to integrate new scientific discoveries with ancient theological understandings of God, incorporating new ways of organizing human society with religious valuing of human life as in the image of God that transcend time and space. Not so long ago, belonging to the church was enough to give a sense of meaning and identity that carried one through childhood and into adulthood. But as historian Philip Sheldrake points out, "Faith is no longer a simple matter of passing a received wisdom from generation to generation."[5] Belonging to a particular denominational institution no longer provides that meaningful structure for many Christians today, and seekers move from one congregation or religion to another in search of the approach—or even a blend of religious traditions—that will "work" for them.

This widespread decline in loyalty to a particular Christian mainline or liturgical denomination has raised troubling visions of failure and loss for many Christians whose beloved churches are shrinking and seen as increasingly irrelevant, but it has also challenged us to take a more honest look at ourselves, asking who we are and what we stand for. What does it mean to be the church, the body of Christ, in the twenty-first century? What do we believe to be true about God, and how and where and in whom is God being revealed today? What is essential, and what can be let go? What needs to change, and what needs to be preserved and valued? How do we retrieve the stories of those who lived in the "shadow side" of history, whose lives or beliefs did not fit with the views of the prevailing institutional powers or dominant culture, and who were therefore silenced or pushed to the margins?

Sheldrake notes that in the life cycle of any spiritual tradition there is a time of breakdown. The original vision seems stale, weighed down by rules and structures; the tradition (or the entire church) is seen as "anachronistic." Sheldrake offers two directions such a tradition might take at this point in its life: renewal or death.

> The spiritual tradition may find its way back to the radical flexibility that characterized the phase of emergence so that a new synthesis between the tradition and its context may emerge. In other words, the tradition rediscovers meaning, renews itself and takes the risk of opening itself up anew to the concrete demands of the gospel in the present. . . . At the other extreme, the inbuilt rigidities of the tradition may lead to resistance and a rejection of the need for flexibility.

There will be an attempt to force the contemporary context or culture back into line with the inherited theory! The result, eventually, will be death.[6]

We see this process of renewal at work in a number of churches today, as we attempt in a variety of ways this "new synthesis" between our inherited past and the present context.

In her book *The Great Emergence*, Phyllis Tickle recalls the image Anglican bishop Mark Dyer has somewhat humorously used to describe this process of reexamination and letting go of patterns of being and praying that no longer fit: "About every five hundred years," Dyer has observed, "the Church feels compelled to hold a giant rummage sale." Tickle agrees with Dyer that we are living through one of those times, and yet any discussion of this emerging life in the church must begin with the past. "Only history can expose the patterns and confluences of the past in such a way as to help us identify the patterns and flow of our own times and occupy them more faithfully." Tickle firmly believes "a more vital form of Christianity" will emerge from this twenty-first-century rummage sale, just as it has in every great time of change and reevaluation in the past—yet even as the "business of any rummage sale [is] first to remove all the old treasures that belonged to one's parents so as to get on with the business of keeping house the new way,"[7] we must have an understanding of the treasured practices and beliefs we are ready to discard. Like those exuberant shoppers on *Antiques Road Show* who are told the encrusted vase they bought at someone's yard sale for a dollar is a Tiffany worth several thousand, we need to know what we have before we let it go.

RE-TRADITIONING THE TRADITION

The Episcopal Church has shared in the experience of being swamped and at times thrown off-course by this postmodern wave of critical reevaluation of religions, but it has also experienced a sense of exhilaration and clarity in learning to navigate the rapids. We have needed to grow strong and courageous enough to let some of our old ways of being and believing and praying die, and to be reborn. In a society that no longer assumes an association with any particular church or religious tradition, we have been forced to examine what we believe and why it matters. As early as 1912, some Episcopalians were seeing this work of clarification and commitment as salutary for the church: "The time will come," warned Vida Scudder, "when the Christian faith will have to fight for right of way among crowding antagonists as vigorously as in the times of Athanasius and Augustine. And in thoughts like these all genuine Christians must rejoice. Without the call to high adventure, the faith has never flourished."[8]

At the same time, we are a church that embraces the past while living in the present and moving into the future: we know that the traditions of Christians who have gone before us in history can offer our postmodern world an enlivening practice of faith, a way of encountering the living God. Phyllis Tickle captures this desire for "re-traditioning" in her engaging image of church members as "fond refurbishers who have inherited a much-loved and historic house":

> They seek to update the wiring, install better plumbing, and modernize the kitchen, but not in order to sell the house. Quite the contrary. They want to live in it for all of time, while simultaneously increasing its comfortableness, enhancing its natural beauty, and exposing its welcoming warmth to all who pass by.[9]

Those who have lived in old houses or worshiped in historic churches know the mixed blessing of aging buildings: they can link us to the past and give us a sense of connectedness to those who lived in their rooms and walked their staircases before us, but they can also weigh us down. Carrying on the traditions of the past constrains the choices of today, and distracts us from the work of moving forward by their need for constant repair and maintenance. "If history gives us a place to stand, a sense of being earthed and grounded, this is not to be confused with being static," writes Benedictine scholar Esther de Waal. "While we need the past we must not let ourselves become imprisoned by it or allow it to become an idol."[10]

As a church that has long valued the creeds and ancient liturgies of earlier times, Episcopalians have struggled with the creative tension of holding the beliefs and practicing the traditions of the past while living thoroughly immersed in the present and open to the future. As theologian Martin Smith notes, "Faithfulness to tradition does not mean mere perpetuation or copying of ways from the past but a creative recovery of the past as a source of inspiration and guidance in our faithfulness to God's future."[11]

This "creative recovery of the past" is not an easy or straightforward undertaking. All history is interpretation, and is conditioned by the cultural, religious, and social context in which it took place. As we seek to recover our roots and draw nourishment from them ourselves, it is tempting to use the past for our own ends, and to see in the words and actions of previous generations the beliefs and models we need to see in our own. We may encounter views about women or people of other races or religions we find distasteful or abhorrent, yet we must let the people of the past speak from within the culture that shaped them—whether we agree with them or not. At the same time, we can also read back in time perhaps too enthusiastically the perspectives we value today, and thus obscure or distort their message unintentionally.

As we undertake a study of spiritual traditions, we will find ourselves attracted to some more than to others; some will resonate with our own experience of God and lead us further on the spiritual path, while others we simply will not understand or see as valuable or perhaps even true. Sheldrake provides several important questions that should be kept in mind when embarking on a study involving a historical account of spirituality:

Who was holy and what was holy?
Who creates or controls spirituality?
What directions were not taken?
Where are the groups that did not fit?

In other words, when we read a certain text or try to understand the characteristics of a particular movement in the church's history, we will always be reading through the lens of that writer or historian. "Taken together," Sheldrake asserts, "these questions focus on one basic issue: the ways in which certain groups become insiders, and others outsiders, in the history of spirituality."[12] Our task in recovering the lively possibilities of ancient traditions, then, involves not just piecing together a patchwork of infinite variety, but also turning the quilt over and trying to discern the design hidden by a silence induced by the dominant culture, as well as being open to the discovery of previously unknown patterns from other cultures and times.

For many Episcopalians it is this lively embrace of tradition that draws many of us to the liturgical churches today. We find an important connection to the life of God through praying liturgies that have been used for centuries, in damp Roman catacombs and medieval monastic stone chapels, in Gothic cathedrals and colonial clapboard congregations, and in modern parish buildings filled with sunlight. The words and gestures and vestments have evolved over the years, adapting to different cultures and different theological sensibilities, but the core shape of how human beings grow in the spiritual life and the foundational truths about God to which these liturgies and traditions of prayer witness has remained recognizable through the ages. It is these ancient yet lively Anglican spiritual traditions that keep drawing us back to the church Sunday after Sunday, day by day, year by year, and sustaining our spiritual growth over the course of our lives.

Christianity as a way of life is what this book is all about: it is the story of individuals and communities who have sought to walk in the light of faith, to live as those who have been filled with the Spirit of God, to be the body of Christ in the world. This way has had any number of twists and turns, and we will follow those traditions that had particular influence on the part of the body of Christ known as Anglicanism, focusing on those that seem to bear most directly on the Episcopal Church today and have the potential for bearing authentic fruit in a new era and a different culture. Participation in the life of a parish church is a source of nourishment for many, and that includes not only sharing in worship and the sacraments, but also studying the Bible and theological writings, maintaining a personal connection to God in prayer, caring for those in need, and working to develop a more just society. Interest in Benedictine spirituality has expanded beyond the monastery walls in recent decades as the need for balance, stability, and a rule of life has intensified. Similarly, the need for authentic community has led to a resurgence of interest in alternative ways of structuring the family and society, in "mixed life" communities and parish groups reminiscent of the Beguines or the community at Little Gidding, groups that follow a common a rule of life while living and working in the world. Some ancient practices, such as regular private confession in the presence of a priest, have been largely neglected or even abandoned by many Episcopalians, while others are seeing renewed life in new forms, as in exploring ways of walking the labyrinth or praying with beads beyond the rosary.

No matter what path our spiritual journey has taken over the course of our lives, or what our particular interests or yearnings for spiritual growth may be, for most of us baptism was the moment at which we began our walk in the Christian way. Since baptism has for two millennia been "the essential foundation on which all Christian life is built,"[13] we will begin our survey of spiritual traditions with that sacrament of new birth. Indeed, our response to the call of baptism articulated in the Baptismal Covenant will shape the chapters of this book and serve as the lens through which we see this ancient and lively story—our story. And so we begin with baptism.

Setting Out

We receive you into the household of God. Confess the faith of Christ crucified, proclaim his resurrection, and share with us in his eternal priesthood. (BCP 308)

> Once I lay in darkness and in the depths of night and was tossed to and fro in the waves of the turbulent world, uncertain of the correct way to go, ignorant of my true life and a stranger to the light of truth. At that time and on account of the life I then led, it seemed difficult to believe what divine mercy promised for my salvation, namely, that someone could be born again and to a new life by being immersed in the healing water of baptism. It was difficult to believe that though I would remain the same man in bodily form, my heart and mind would be transformed. How was it possible, I thought, that a change could be great enough to strip away in a single moment the innate hardness of our nature? How could the habits acquired over the course of many years disappear, since these are so deeply rooted within us?[1]

These words from a third-century bishop of Carthage give voice to both the hopes and the doubts many modern Christians hold about the power of baptism in our lives. We are told that in the waters of baptism we are born to new life in Jesus Christ, that our sins are forgiven, that we are welcomed into the household of God. And yet many of us do not remember our baptisms as infants, and as adults we, like Cyprian, wonder how a few drops of water could wash away "the innate hardness of our nature" and erase the deeply rooted habits of a lifetime. We also share the questions Cyprian expressed about his experience of God: how do we find the "new life," the healing and wholeness promised in the waters of baptism? How do we know the "correct way to go"? How do we find light in the midst of much that is dark in our world?

For Cyprian, who was baptized as an adult, the grace of baptism itself provided some of the answers to his questions. "After the life-giving water of baptism came to my rescue," he wrote, "and took away the stain of my former years and poured into my cleansed and purified heart the light which comes from above, and after I had drunk in the Heavenly Spirit and was made a new man by a second birth, then amazingly what I had previously doubted became clear to me. What had been hidden was revealed. What had been dark became light. What previously had seemed impossible now seemed possible." In his experience of baptism Cyprian knew that "what was made alive in me by the Holy Spirit was now quickened by God."

While this experience of clarity and hope, faith and light was focused for Cyprian in his moment of baptism, for many of us today these experiences of God are part of the ongoing journey of faith that begins with our baptism but whose meaning is understood only through our daily living within "the household of God." In a modern-day baptismal creed, the Australian priest John Gaden strikes a thoroughly contemporary but similar note in his deeply personal experience of coming to faith in Christ. "What is it that obscures the light in me?" he asks himself.

> My failures. Knowing what I should do, the love I should have for people, I just can't rise to it. Other forces seem to tie me down. The darkness is outside and in. But I hate evil. I am against repression, the restrictions that destroy people's lives. I renounce the powers of darkness. I stand looking at the dark, and turn away to face the Light.

Gaden goes on to reflect on the reasons why it is so crucial for him to turn away from his old life and "face the light"—reasons drawn from his reverence for nature, from his experience of human and divine love, and from the gift of community.

> The Voice asks, "What do you believe? On what do you stand against the dark?" In springtime, I have seen a daffodil unfold, the pale yellow petals burst from their green sheaths. At the tips of branches I have seen buds, pregnant with life, ready to spring forth. I put my hand to my heart and listen to the dull, pulsating beat driving the blood of life through me. I am alive, I have life. Again, I've looked up and seen a bird drifting in the wind, or at evening sat and watched the sun, a huge red ball, go down upon the sea. So I affirm, this world is good. Despite all the darkness of evil, I belong here. My life is a gracious gift, given me to live. I will be baptized in the name of the Father, Creator of heaven and earth.
>
> But there is more than the living, physical world of beauty. I take my stand on love, the depths of love that forgives and accepts me, love that gives itself for others, love that is stronger than death, the love that I see around me in children, women and men, but most clearly in Jesus. I will be baptized in the name of the Son, Jesus Christ our Lord.
>
> As well as love, I believe in a creative spirit, the enthusiasm of the young with their hopes and dreams, the creativity of artists, writers, musicians, poets. There is a spirit, too, which ties together those with a common purpose, families, groups, the spirit of unity, the spirit of humanity. I will be baptized in the Name of the Holy Spirit.

Like Cyprian, John Gaden also writes of his baptismal cleansing as an overwhelming experience of grace and renewal; for him it was a time of standing at the abyss of the darkness of death, "on the brink of the void of nothingness," and knowing he is alive:

> Now I am washed clean. I have stepped out of the bath. I smell with the perfume of fragrant oil. White clothes, clean and fresh,

cover me. The dawn is breaking outside, and the first fingers of light spread across the sky. I feel new, made whole. My life has meaning. The darkness has been washed away. I have seen the darkness of death, the gloom of despair. I have stood on the brink of the void of nothingness, but I am alive. Nothing can terrify me now, neither death nor prison, neither earthquake nor sin. I am Christ's and Christ is mine. Nothing can separate me from his life and love. His Spirit is with us, refreshing, comforting, insistently urging us to live.[2]

These experiences of God's grace may sound familiar to you, though you may not have experienced it at the moment of your baptism. Many of us have come to faith in the God who is "insistently urging us to live" by different paths, and we might not describe our experience of or belief about God in exactly the same words as John Gaden or Cyprian. Yet however God has led us toward a life of faith, for most Christians the path generally starts at the door of baptism.

Since we are baptized only once in our lives, and often the rite took place when we were infants, the meaning of our baptism must often be discovered in hindsight. It can seem a daunting task, and we may even wonder why it matters at all. Baptism matters not because we are denied the saving grace of God without it, but because, as one writer has put it, baptism is "the moment when our feet are set on that path." Our baptism makes us part of the church, incorporating us into the body of Christ and endowing us with the Holy Spirit, "which binds us together as the communion of saints."[3] Baptism is thus both the start of a journey, and a moment to which we return as a plumb line and guide throughout our lives. It is a sacrament of identity, the beginning of an ongoing relationship with God in Christ within the Christian community. It is thus an identity we can remember and claim at various times throughout our lives. In this sense, our baptism is always fresh, always contemporary, always open to new and deeper meaning in our lives.

Such opportunities to renew and reclaim our experience of baptism are given to us at every turn in worship: when we stand to reaffirm our faith in God in the words of the creed, when we pray in the midst of the Christian community for those in need, when we confess our sins and return to the God who has forgiven us, when we receive the bread and wine of the eucharist. And as we shall see, that renewal and reclamation of our baptism also extends beyond our worship and into the daily fabric of our lives, as we come to know the power of the Spirit who has been given to us in baptism and abides with us forever. The Anglican spiritual practices of the Christian life we will consider in this book all find their origin and their end in baptism: our beliefs, prayer, and study, our repentance and confession, our loving service to others, our concern for the common good—all are practiced because of our baptism, because we have been given new life as members of the body of Christ. The Christian identity given to us in our baptism compels us to practice the faith that is in us, and leads us through that practice back to a deeper understanding of what it means to be a baptized Christian, a "little Christ."

What Is Baptism?

The shape and meaning of Christian baptism has changed and evolved over the centuries since Jesus was baptized in the Jordan River, and its meaning to each of us individually may well change over the course of our lifetime. Baptism is a sacrament with multiple meanings, and whether it is understood in terms of new birth, the forgiveness of sins, dying and rising in Christ, or becoming part of the Christian community, its primary purpose is initiation into a new identity, a new way of being. Baptism is not merely "a rite performed at the beginning of one's Christian life," liturgist Louis Weil reminds us, but instead creates "an abiding context within which we live out the whole of our lives in Christ. Our daily life in Christ is the living out of our baptism, as we grow ever more deeply into our baptismal identity."[4] When we experience grief and loss, for example, our belief in the communion of saints that holds all our souls in this life and the life to come may be our only light in the darkness. When our actions have offended or injured someone we love, the baptismal call to practice repentance and to depend on the forgiveness of sins may bring us steady comfort and a way to repair the relationship. When we witness an occasion in which justice is not served because of prejudice or callous indifference, our efforts to practice fairness and kindness in our everyday lives may make a real difference to others. In these and countless other ways, our baptismal identity shapes and forms our spiritual practice as Christians throughout our lives.

In the New Testament the primary meaning of baptism seems to be the forgiveness of sins, though the baptismal rites and catechetical instruction varied from region to region: as historian Paul Bradshaw has noted, "Jesus apparently did not leave his followers with a fixed set of doctrines but rather with an experience that changed their lives, which they then tried to articulate in their own ways." We thus find that in the New Testament these earliest disciples espoused "not one standard theology of baptism or a systematized explanation of what it means to become a Christian, but a variety of ways of speaking about that experience," with very different images and metaphors used by different writers.[5] For example, John the Baptist preached a baptism of repentance, perhaps in the context of Jewish proselyte baptism. While the early Christians abandoned the need for circumcision of Gentile converts, they held on to the practice of baptism as a means of turning from the way of sin and death, and confessing one's faith in Jesus Christ as Lord.

The earliest preparation for Christian baptism focused on conversion from Judaism or paganism, with most of the converts being adults or entire households. The language of the baptismal rites spoke of renouncing evil and idolatry, of moving from slavery to sin into the freedom of the children of God, of enlightenment and rebirth, or regeneration. Immersion in cold, "living" water such as a river or lake seemed to be the normal expectation, though the early teaching in the *Didache* concedes that "if you do not have living water, baptize in other water; if you cannot in cold, then in warm; if you do not have either, pour water three times on the head in the name of Father, Son, and Holy Spirit." The confession of one's faith was a central part of the rite: the statement of faith known to us today as the Apostles' Creed was originally the threefold baptismal affirmation of one's belief in God the Father, God the Son, and God the Holy Spirit.

During this early time in the life of the church there were two clear stages in the process of initiation: a period of varying length that focused on the moral dimensions of the gospel as these were expressed in the candidate's life and actions, followed by a brief, formal period of candidacy immediately prior to baptism, in which the candidate was instructed in the Christian faith and life. One early document known as the *Apostolic Tradition* describes a three-year period of preparation known as the catechumenate, during which one's entire life came under scrutiny and was brought into the light of Christian faith. Sometimes lives were completely disrupted; catechumens had to rethink all aspects of their routines, their relationships, and their daily work. They could not practice occupations that involved immorality or the exercise of force (such as serving in the military), for example, or that were associated with the pagan cults of the Roman empire, whether in political roles or through teaching in schools. The practice of pagan religions affected every aspect of life in Roman society: marriage, family and household, economic and political life. Baptism into the Christian faith could entail a complete and even devastating breaking of ties to one's family and to one's entire past in order to give allegiance to Christ.

As Christianity spread beyond the Jewish community in Palestine throughout the Roman empire, it remained a persecuted sect until 313, when the emperor Constantine legalized Christian worship with his Edict of Milan, which declared "it was proper that the Christians and all others should have liberty to follow that mode of religion which to each of them appeared best," thus granting tolerance to all religious practices and sects of the empire. As Christians were no longer marginalized, imprisoned, or martyred for their faith, the church began to take root and flourish in Roman society, attracting large numbers of converts. Some of these "newcomers" came for reasons of faith, convinced by the preaching of salvation and new life; some came out of curiosity about this new religion. Others joined the church in order to marry a Christian, seek public office, or gain lucrative financial contracts and business connections.

A newly legalized Christianity had its own challenges and stresses, however, as churches were flooded with adult converts seeking admission, and baptismal preparation could no longer be done as carefully or individually as before. Teaching and preparation for baptism now had to be offered for large groups of candidates with differing backgrounds and varying levels of commitment. During the fourth century, the Easter Vigil became the preferred time for these group baptisms in the church because of its powerful images of death and resurrection. The forty days of fasting prior to baptism created the season of Lent, weeks that preceded the vigil and were an intensive time of final teaching on the creed and Christian faith that culminated in baptism.

The fourth century thus saw a flourishing of catechetical instruction to meet the needs of many different kinds of converts. The sermons of the leading bishops of the time, such as Ambrose of Milan, Cyril of Jerusalem, John Chrysostom in Antioch, and Theodore of Mopsuestia, give insight into the supreme importance of baptism in the life of the fourth-century church and the reverence in which it was held. "Baptism is a burial and a resurrection," Cyril of Jerusalem told his congregation. "In the same moment you were both dying and being born, and that water of salvation was at once your grave and your mother."[6] In this fundamental human mystery of birth and burial, life and death we experience one of the profound meanings of Christian baptism: the hope that "if we have been united with him in a death like his, we will certainly be united with him in a resurrection like his" (Rom. 6:5).

Theodore of Mopsuestia likewise described baptism as a powerful "working of the Holy Spirit" and occasion of grace. "The power of the holy baptism consists in this," he taught his catechumens. "It implants in you the hope of future benefits, enables you to participate in the things which we expect, and by means of the symbols and signs of the future good things, it informs you with the gift of the Holy Spirit the firstfruits of whom you receive when you are baptized."[7] In this description of baptism as both a doorway to hope that opens new possibilities for the future and an indwelling of the Holy Spirit who empowers and enlivens our souls, we hear echoes of Cyprian's experience of baptism as a grace-filled moment of clarity and promise, and of John Gaden's affirmation that all of the good things of life lead us to a belief in God.

While many of us today would call our experience of baptism unremarkable if not entirely lost to memory, for many fourth-century Christians the baptismal rite would have been unforgettable—and intentionally so. After weeks or months of preparation and teaching, the candidates arrived at the church on the night before Easter. During the vigil they were taken to the nearby baptistery, where they promised to renounce evil and affirmed their belief in the God of Jesus Christ, stripped off their clothes, and allowed themselves to be immersed—drowned—in the waters of baptism. As they rose again from the waters, they were dried, anointed with oil, and dressed in the white robes of the newly baptized.

Although the practice of anointing with oil in baptism varied from time to time and place to place, in many early liturgies the priest would mark the forehead of the newly baptized with the sign of the cross. This act of signing with oil could convey the sense of "branding" the new Christian as one of God's own, as when converts to Judaism would be marked at baptism with the Taw (T), the last letter of the Hebrew alphabet, to signify being marked with the name of God. The Taw came to be interpreted by Christians as the sign of the cross, and in devotional practice the making of the sign of the cross served as a reminder of one's baptism. The common practice of calling the baptism a "christening" is linked to this anointing with oil: "christen" comes from the word "chrism," and to be "christened" is to be "anointed."[8]

John Chrysostom describes what would happen next in his congregations:

> As soon as they came forth from those sacred waters, all who are present embrace them, greet them, kiss them, rejoice with them, and congratulate them, because those who were heretofore slaves and captives have suddenly become free men and sons and have been invited to the royal table. For straightaway

after they come up from the waters, they are led to the awesome
table heavy laden with countless flavours where they taste of the
Master's body and blood, and become a dwelling place for the
Holy Spirit.[9]

We see in Chrysostom's description the importance of baptism
as a communal sacrament, for it was initiation into the Christian
community, the body of Christ. He also makes explicit the link
between baptism and the eucharist in the early church. In a recent
essay Louis Weil reminds us that in the early church the receiving
of the consecrated bread and wine was understood to be the *completion* of baptism: the eucharist was experienced as "the ongoing
and repeatable part of initiation," as well as "a constant reminder
of the identity which baptism had created."[10] It is in this sense that
we today "practice baptism" and deepen our understanding of its
meaning in our lives every time we gather at the altar to share in
the bread and wine. In the receiving of the body and blood of
Christ we affirm our baptismal identity as members of his body. In
the often quoted words of Augustine, in the eucharist we behold
what we are and become what we receive, the body of Christ.[11]

Just as the mystery of the eucharist is experienced in the eating of bread and drinking of wine, the symbols of baptism are
similarly rooted in the stuff of ordinary life. The baptismal rites
that developed in the first four centuries of the church may seem
esoteric to us, but they were in fact linked with the ordinary bath-
ing habits of the time, when communal baths were the norm. The
practice of anointing with oil was familiar both to Jewish converts
who knew of the tradition of anointing their kings and to Gentiles
who attended sporting events in which athletes were rubbed with
oil to enhance their performance. The branding of a mark on the
foreheads of slaves was familiar to those in commerce, as a sign
of ownership or allegiance. In other words, new Christians could
understand these rites because they were linked with social and
cultural practices they already knew: the actions in the baptismal
liturgy of kneeling and rising again, of stretching one's arms toward
heaven, of turning one's body toward the east or west, of dressing
and undressing, of descending into and rising from the water—all

were familiar actions in ordinary daily life, though they were filled with new meaning in the baptismal rite.

While many of these aspects of the ritual have been retained or restored in recent revisions of the Book of Common Prayer, some will have more meaning than others for our own culture. And this specificity within the culture is as it should be, as Daniel Stevick has noted so well: "Baptism is a wet, earthy act, involving people in relation to one another, bodies acting and touching one another, hands, clothing, oil, light, and eating and drinking. It is often emotion filled. Baptism would not be more true to itself in some disembodied form." While baptism itself may be a universal practice in the church, the specific form it takes in a particular church will be shaped by the people and society in which it is practiced, and "thus it will use the materials and take on the style of the culture in a very considerable measure."[12]

In the Episcopal Church this has sometimes meant a loss in the intensity of the symbols of baptism as we have sought to adjust to the sensibilities of the culture. Thus we have replaced cold, living water in a communal bath with lukewarm water in a bowl, drawn from the tap, and we use only a smidgeon of oil to anoint the forehead. And yet with the 1979 prayer book baptism has been recovered from its private chapel and brought into a central place in Sunday worship, and in the Easter Vigil the ancient baptismal symbols may be recovered and their meaning experienced afresh. Louis Weil tells the story of hearing an audible gasp from the congregation as he poured an entire vial of oil over the head of a candidate for baptism. Yet as the fragrance of the oil suffused the church, he could feel a powerful awareness of the deeper meaning of anointing also filling the congregation. "Not a word of explanation was needed," Weil concluded; "the entire community smelled the fragrance of Christ."[13]

New Occasions, New Meanings

From the fifth century on through the middle ages, the sacramental practice of baptism became focused on the initiation of infants and on the conversion of entire groups and populations as a result of the territorial expansion of Christendom. One factor was the increasing popularity of the doctrine of what came to be called "original sin"—the belief that all human beings bear the mark of Adam's fall from a state of grace, and therefore even infants are guilty of sin and must be baptized in order to save them from eternal damnation. Another was the high rates of infant mortality. In any case, the age of candidates for baptism decreased until it was customary for infants to be baptized as soon as possible after birth. By the eighth century in the west, we see baptismal liturgies that simply assume the candidates will be infants, some even with rubrics indicating the babies are not to be nursed during the liturgy in the time between the water baptism and its completion later in the service by the reception of communion.

As Christian missionaries spread northward into northern Europe and the British Isles, moreover, the baptism of entire tribes or peoples would follow the conversion of a king or tribal leader. These wholesale baptisms were often performed with little or no instruction or meaningful affirmation of faith; instead they were political alliances or submission by conquered peoples. These were justified by the expectation that, over time, genuine beliefs and religious practices would gradually take root among the people and grow into authentic faith—or at the very least a cultural acceptance of Christian social and moral principles as interpreted by the given culture of the missionaries. The hope of conversion was also often held out as a reason for military advances against neighboring peoples.

A sixth-century history of the consolidation of the tribes of Gaul into the kingdom of the Franks, written by Gregory of Tours, gives us a glimpse of how the practice of baptism in the early medieval period could be both a personal affirmation of faith and a political tool for the establishment of governmental authority. In his chapter on the conversion of the Frankish king Clovis, Gregory describes how Clovis's wife, Clotilda, pleaded with her husband to baptize their infant son:

> She tried unceasingly to persuade her husband, saying: "The gods you worship are nothing, and they will be unable to help themselves or any one else. For they are graven out of stone or wood or some metal. And the names you have given them are

names of men and not of gods. . . . They are endowed rather with the magic arts than with the power of the divine name. But he ought rather to be worshipped who created by his word heaven and earth, the sea and all that in them is out of a state of nothingness, who made the sun shine, and adorned the heavens with stars, who filled the waters with creeping things, the earth with living things and the air with creatures that fly, at whose nod the earth is decked with growing crops, the trees with fruit, the vines with grapes, by whose hand mankind was created, by whose generosity all that creation serves and helps man whom he created as his own."[14]

Clotilda's words fell on deaf ears, but she nonetheless prepared her son for baptism and decorated the church, "in order that he who could not moved by persuasion might be urged to belief by this mystery." Tragically, the son died immediately after being baptized, still clothed in his white baptismal garments, and an enraged Clovis berated the queen and saw in the death an affirmation that his gods were in fact more powerful than hers. Clotilda, who saw the matter rather differently, retorted that she was did not grieve for her son, because she knew that, "summoned from this world as he was in his baptismal garments, he will be fed by the vision of God."

Clovis and Clotilda continued to debate the superior power and truth of each other's gods until Clovis was in a tight fix during a war with another tribe, in the course of which his army was in danger of being destroyed. When Clovis realized the impending disaster, he burst into tears and prayed to Jesus Christ, "whom Clotilda asserts to be the son of the living God" and who is "said to give aid to those in distress, and to bestow victory on those who hope in thee." Clovis begged for help in his battle, and promised that if God would grant him victory and let him "know that power which she says that people dedicated in thy name have had from thee," then he would believe and be baptized in Christ's name. "For I have invoked my own gods," Clovis ruefully concluded, "but, as I find, they have withdrawn from aiding me; and therefore I believe that they possess no power, since they do not help those who obey them. I now call upon thee, I desire to believe thee, only let me be rescued from my adversaries." After his prayer Clovis discovered his enemies were fleeing and their king had been killed; when they had surrendered and Clovis returned home in peace, he "told the queen how he had had merit to win the victory by calling on the name of Christ."

This victory was followed by Clovis's baptism by Remigius, bishop of Rheims, along with three thousand of his soldiers. After his conversion Clovis continued his vigorous quest to conquer all the peoples of the land, this time with a different god on his side, telling his people, "I take it very hard that these Arians [Christians who did not believe in the divinity of Jesus] hold part of the Gauls. Let us go with God's help and conquer them and bring the land under our control." Various signs and answers to prayer aided their efforts, according to Gregory's account, and the tribes in the area were brought to submission "by God's aid," though with great bloodshed and loss of life, allowing Clovis to crown himself as king of the Franks.

In this historical account of the uniting of the peoples of Gaul into a single kingdom under a Christian king, we see only one example of how baptism and faith in the middle ages were in many cases inextricably tied with military conquest. Victory or defeat in battle was reason enough to turn from other local gods to the God of the Christian faith. The earlier emphasis on individual catechesis and adult affirmation of faith was in many cases lost in the desire to "convert" entire peoples for purposes of stability and political unification.

This pattern of using baptismal practice as a way of initiating (willingly or unwillingly) others into both the Christian faith and a particular culture fell into disuse once the boundaries of a European Christendom were settled, but it would be repeated whenever the missionaries or armies of a Christian country travelled to other lands to establish colonies, or encountered other native peoples within their borders. The compilers of the 1662 Book of Common Prayer, for example, included a new liturgy of baptism "for those of riper years" to address in part the needs of American colonists who were converting and baptizing the Native Americans they met there. In recent decades this practice has come under healthy scrutiny and rejected by many Anglicans, especially when these baptisms involved the destruction or suppression of native communities, cultures, and beliefs.

For a great majority of Christians from the middle ages on, however, the sacrament of baptism was simply the accepted practice of parents who were expected to incorporate their infants into the life of the church. The Roman rite became the prevailing pattern for baptism: in 789 Charlemagne ordered it to be used throughout his empire, and a century before, Augustine of Canterbury brought it to Britain. Regional variations in practice continued to develop; it was the Sarum rite from Salisbury Cathedral, which was in common use in England, Wales, and Ireland until the 1500s, that formed the basis for Anglican baptismal liturgies after the Reformation.

Although the reformers criticized the practice of baptizing children with a Latin rite spoken in a near-empty church, which made it difficult to affirm the importance of such a commitment in the life of a Christian, most retained the practice of infant baptism. Despite the instruction in the 1549 prayer book that baptisms were to be administered on "Sundays and other holy days when the most number of people may come together," in practice baptisms continued to be done quietly and in private, as this description by William Sherlock of St. Paul's Church in London, written in 1682, attests:

> Public baptism is now very much grown out of fashion; most people look upon it as a very needless and troublesome ceremony, to carry their children to the public congregation, there to be solemnly admitted into the fellowship of Christ's church. They think it may be as well done in a private chamber, as soon as the child is born, with little company and with little noise.[15]

Those Episcopalians who have been raised with the 1979 Book of Common Prayer's theology of the centrality of baptism in the life of the church might find William Sherlock's assessment of baptism as a "very needless and troublesome ceremony" better performed "in a private chamber" somewhat quaint and even amusing. Yet in many parishes our actual *practice* of baptism is still rather like that experience of St. Paul's London. Since 1979, baptisms have been brought into the congregation's worship on Sunday morning, but it is not always clear that rigorous or even minimal preparation of the candidates and their families regarding the Christian faith and significance of baptism has been done. Nor is it always clear what exactly is meant by the commitment of the people in the congregation witnessing the baptismal vows "to do all in their power" to support the candidates in their new life in Christ (BCP 303). Many longtime and faithful churchgoers may not actually know what this promise entails. These are spiritual practices of catechesis and community life that continue to evolve in the Episcopal Church, as we live into new meanings and models of baptism for the life of the church in the twenty-first century.

For example, infant baptism may be a helpful practice for families who wish to incorporate a newly born child into their life of faith. During times of social stability in a culture, notes Daniel Stevick, baptism simply does "its quiet work of witnessing to the continuity of the generations in the age-old people of God. It is a mark of a faith held and handed on from generation to generation, reverently and little changed, like life itself."[16] Yet as more and more children are raised in families that do not practice a religious faith, the need for creative and thoughtful catechesis of older children and adults becomes more pressing.

"AN ORDINATION OF THE LAITY"

The recovery of baptism as the central and universal act of initiation into the church holds great power, both for bringing about and for interpreting the changes taking place in the church and in human lives today. We may understand baptism as a call to a deeper faith, "a divine summons to stand forth from the casually believing crowd" that we hear days, months, or even years after the day the water was actually poured over our heads. This call may be heard at a time of spiritual crisis when matters of faith take on an imperative they have not had before, or simply in a time of awakening to faith in the course of searching for meaning in one's daily life. But however and whenever it is heard, the call of baptism is not just to an affirmation of faith; it is also a commissioning for ministry that might be called an "ordination of the laity." Baptism not only provides strength for the spiritual struggle throughout one's life, it also brings us into the communion of Christ's church: it "sets one within the people of God, the holy priesthood; it brings one into the eucharistic fellowship."[17] These are the enduring commitments of baptism at any age, and we will spend a lifetime entering into the mystery of living them fully and completely in our daily lives.

We learn the significance of our baptism only by practicing the faith into which the baptismal rite initiates us, and the questions of the Baptismal Covenant in the prayer book can provide a helpful framework for that practice, as we seek to live out our commitment to the Christian faith and life. The five questions of the Baptismal Covenant in the 1979 Book of Common Prayer are new to this edition. They are an expansion and interpretation in modern language and sensibilities of a question that was added to the baptismal rite of the 1662 prayer book by Robert Sanderson, later bishop of Lincoln, during a time when its use was forbidden by the government. The question followed the renunciations of evil and the affirmation of faith, and asked: "Wilt thou then obediently keep God's holy will and commandments, and walk in the same all the days of thy life?"

These five questions of the Baptismal Covenant explore the five areas of Christian living, revealing the landscape in which faith unfolds. First, Christians live in *community*, even when they experience physical solitude. This community life involves teaching and learning, sharing in the bread and wine of Christ's body, and praying for others, for the church, for the world, for one's own salvation and wholeness.

Second, Christians develop the discernment to recognize evil and the courage to resist it. They learn to see and "name" all that draws them away from God, and when they fall into sin, they choose to repent and return to the Lord. In Anglican tradition this awareness of the need for ongoing conversion has been expressed in terms of *sanctification*, especially through the sacraments, and growth in a life of holiness through daily prayer.

Third, Christians offer witness to the Good News by both *word and example*. The study of Scripture and the practice of faith are inseparable in Anglicanism, which has a rich tradition of learning and literature that yearns to be shared with others.

Fourth, Christians live a life of *service*, seeking and serving Christ in all persons. This service is offered in a multitude of ways, from the church's ministries of pastoral care and outreach to the daily care of others practiced by individual Christians in the home, workplace, and marketplace. The Benedictine tradition is of particular influence in its emphasis on hospitality and the structuring of a communal life that benefits all.

And fifth, the Christian life involves a commitment to work for *justice and peace* among all people, and thereby to respect the dignity of every person. In Anglicanism this call to justice and peace has taken many forms, including efforts to abolish slavery, to provide a more just and equitable distribution of the world's economic wealth, and to uphold the equal human rights of all people.

Each of the following chapters will address one of these aspects of the Christian life, exploring in particular how Anglicans have sought to live out their baptismal vows through the centuries and explaining the spiritual practices that have helped them understand this identity as members of the body of Christ. And so we begin with the life of prayer and belief.

ANGLICAN VOICES ON BAPTISM

> Our baptism is to signify our seeking and obtaining a new birth. And our being baptized in, or into the name of the Father, Son and Holy Ghost, tells us in the plainest manner, what birth it is that we seek, namely, such a new birth as may make us again what we were at first, a living real image or offspring of the Father, Son, and Holy Ghost.
>
> —William Law, *A Practical Treatise upon Christian Perfection* (1726)

If God had not intended that women should use their reason, He would not have given them any, for He does nothing in vain. If they are to use their reason, certainly it ought to be employed about the noblest objects, and in business of the greatest consequence, therefore, in religion. That our Godfathers and Godmothers answer'd for us at the font, was an act of charity in them, and will be a great benefit to us if we make a right use of it; but it will be our own condemnation if we are Christians merely upon this account, for that only can be imputed to a free agent which is done with understanding and choice. A Christian woman therefore must not be a child in understanding; she must serve God with understanding as well as with affection; must love Him with all her mind and soul, as well as with all her heart and strength; in a word, must perform a reasonable service if she means to be acceptable to her maker.

—Mary Astell, *The Christian Religion as Profess'd by a Daughter of the Church of England* (1705)

We who call ourselves Christian are members of the church by virtue of our baptism, and we belong to the church for the duration of our lives. Our only decision, therefore, is how to live out or not to live out this belonging; we can do nothing about its reality. Our individual choices for action will be related to our own gifts and graces and to the particular opportunities for faithful response each of us is afforded because of circumstance or position. We can identify various faithful responses and then choose among them, using our own power and authority as God wills for us to do.

Followers of Jesus can choose how to take up their responsibility—their authority—to and for the communities to which they belong. They can adopt one or a combination of these responses, all of which are good and right and are mutually dependent on the others for the church's radical response to the needs of God's created order. These responses can shape and inform each other if taken together. A healthy church living in relationship to the whole of creation—God's company—will be about its mission to love the world that God loves so much.

—Caroline Westerhoff, *Calling: A Song for
the Baptized* (1994)

QUESTIONS FOR REFLECTION AND DISCUSSION

1. What was your baptism like? How were you prepared for the event? If you were an infant, what stories have you been told about your baptism? If you are not baptized, what was your experience of religious or spiritual formation as a child?

2. How have your understandings of baptism changed over time? Which understandings of baptism in church tradition mean the most to you now? Why?

3. If you were to prepare for and plan your baptism now, what would that "catechumenal process" look like? Who would be involved in the preparation? What would the liturgy be like? What symbols of baptismal faith and new life would you include?

Praying Shapes Believing

Will you continue in the apostles' teaching and fellowship, in the breaking of bread, and in the prayers? (BCP 304)

In those days came the murderous persecution to England from the wicked emperor, and the murderers seized the Christians everywhere with exceeding fury; then a priest escaped from them who ran secretly to Alban's house, and there lay hid from his fierce persecutors, and Alban received him, though he was not baptized. Then began the priest, as he loved God, to sing his offices, and fast strictly, and day and night to praise his Lord, and meanwhile to teach the true faith to the honourable Alban, until he believed in the true God, and renounced heathenism, and became a true Christian, and exceeding full of faith. Then the priest dwelt with the honourable man until the magistrate who persecuted the Christians discovered him there, and with great wrath commanded him to be fetched before him speedily.

Then came the messengers to Alban's house, but Alban went out unto the persecutors with the priest's cloak, as if he were he, and would not betray him to the wicked persecutors. He was thereupon bound, and brought straightway to the impious judge, where he was offering to his gods the devilish sacrifices, with all his associates. Then became the judge fiendishly angry, as soon as he beheld the steadfast martyr, because he had received the fugitive priest, and given himself up to be slain for him. . . .

Then asked the judge immediately, and said, "Of what family are you, or of what rank among men?" Then Alban answered
the wicked man thus: "Of what concern is it to you, of what
family I may be? But if you desire to hear the truth, I tell you
quickly that I am a Christian, and will ever worship Christ."

The judge said to him: "Tell me your name, without any
delay, now that I thus ask." The champion of God said to the
murderer thus, "I am hight Albanus, and I believe in the Sav-
iour, who is the true God, and made all creatures; to Him I
pray, and Him will I ever worship."[1]

There are times in our lives when what we believe quietly in our
hearts must be brought to the light and expressed publicly and
without equivocation or delay. Baptism can be one of those times,
or the moment may arise less formally in the midst of an honest
conversation. I recall my grandmother's clear and certain affirmation of her faith in Jesus Christ in response to my searching questions and doubts, as we sat together on an old picnic bench by
their farmhouse in Oklahoma, on a hot, windy day one summer.
"He is as real to me as this table," she said, vigorously tapping the
worn boards with her finger.

For Alban and many other Christians throughout the centuries, the crucial moment of affirmation came during periods
of political or religious persecution, when beliefs that differed
from the prevailing or legalized religion were punished by
fines or torture, imprisonment or death. The first centuries of
Christianity are marked by such times of intense persecution,
depending on who was the Roman emperor at the time; many
Christians, such as Alban and his executioner who, refusing to
kill such a holy man, was beheaded beside him, were "baptized
with their blood."

We value the separation of church and state and a measure
of religious toleration today, which gives us the freedom to live
out our faith quietly and peaceably among those whose religious
beliefs differ from our own. And yet the question of the Baptismal Covenant we are considering here calls us not just to an
affirmation of our belief in God, but a practice of our faith. The

first of the five questions posed in the Baptismal Covenant, following the Apostles' Creed, asks us not *what* we believe—that has just been affirmed in our creedal responses to the questions of who God is—but whether we will *continue* in the practice of that faith within the Christian community. The language of the question is relational rather than doctrinal; it asks us to maintain a living fellowship with the apostles and to follow their teaching, all in the context of communion in a shared meal and a life of daily prayer.

FELLOWSHIP, BREAD, AND PRAYER

The words for this question in the covenant are taken directly from a passage in the Acts of the Apostles, in which Luke describes the very early community life of the followers of the risen Jesus:

> So those who welcomed [Peter's] message were baptized, and that day about three thousand persons were added. They devoted themselves to the apostles' teaching and fellowship, to the breaking of bread and the prayers. Awe came upon everyone, because many wonders and signs were being done by the apostles. All who believed were together and had all things in common; they would sell their possessions and goods and distribute the proceeds to all, as any had need. Day by day, as they spent much time together in the temple, they broke bread at home and ate their food with glad and generous hearts, praising God and having the goodwill of all the people. And day by day the Lord added to their number those who were being saved. (Acts 2:41–47)

They devoted themselves to the apostles' teaching and fellowship, to the breaking of bread and the prayers. For early converts to the Christian faith, the apostles were the twelve disciples who had been followers of Jesus, who had accompanied him as he preached and taught in their synagogues and on the hillsides, in public marketplaces and in private homes. They were the ones who had listened to his words and witnessed his acts of healing; they had shared bread with him at supper and endured the night of betrayal and death. They had seen him alive again, and knew his living presence continued among them in the Holy Spirit. They had come to believe Jesus was indeed more than a prophet, more than a good man—he was the Messiah, the Son of God, the Savior for whom they had been waiting with a longing hope. The apostles were the living witnesses to a Messiah they had seen with their eyes, had touched with their hands, had heard with their ears; and as the "messengers" of God, their ongoing connection to the risen Christ continued his ministry of healing and forgiveness in the working of "wonders and signs" and offering of salvation to all who came to them in hope and heard their message.

Yet almost immediately the Christian community was faced with the question of what was actually meant by "the apostles' teaching and fellowship." Paul boldly called himself an apostle, though he freely admitted he was not one of the original disciples who had accompanied Jesus during his earthly ministry and was "the least of the apostles" because he had once persecuted the church (1 Cor. 15:8–10). Other itinerant teachers and evangelists also came to be viewed as apostles, witnessing to the faith as they visited house churches throughout the Roman empire, but often bringing differing and even contradictory interpretations and practices of that faith. The idealism and generous unity of the first Christian communities Luke describes in Acts quickly deteriorated: the letters of Paul bear witness to the different points of view that created conflict and even chaos within a single community, as well as between groups of local churches. Some of these differences were theological, and expressed a variety of understandings of who Jesus was and the nature of his relation to God; others had more to do with cultural and social customs that conflicted with the religious practices of Palestinian Jewish Christians of that time. "When we listen attentively to the ancient Christians," note two historians of the early church, "we do not, then, hear a single people speaking as if with one voice. Rather, our ears are filled with a multitude of voices, some synchronizing harmoniously, some clamoring contentiously, some simply following their own scripts as if oblivious to the strikingly different words issuing from other quarters."[2]

While there seems to have been a relative tolerance for diversity of belief and practice in the earliest decades of the church's life, as time passed the apostles and teachers who knew Jesus firsthand died out. As new apostles and teachers rose to take their place, invariably the message would be communicated differently, with new perspectives on the oral and written tradition of hymns and prayers, letters and sermons that had been handed on to them. Even in the four gospels in our New Testament, composed near the end of the first century and into the second, we see different understandings and memories of Jesus. As Christianity spread beyond the Jewish world of Palestine, it encountered Roman philosophies such as Platonism and Stoicism along with gnostic teachings on the superiority of spirit to flesh. Converts from these and other religious traditions naturally interpreted the gospel in light of their beliefs and cultural assumptions. How were second-century Christians to evaluate the truth of these new teachings? It could be hard to distinguish the subtle theological differences between gnostic teachers, who purported to have "secret knowledge" of spiritual truths, and orthodox teachers—both of whom affirmed faith in Jesus as Lord, yet might have very different understandings of what happened at the resurrection or how Jesus could be both human and divine.

Ignatius, bishop of Antioch at the end of the first century, wrote of this confusion to the church in the city of Tralles, in Asia Minor, urging them to "use Christian nourishment only," and to abstain from "herbage of a different kind" made by those who "mix up Jesus Christ with their own poison, speaking things that are unworthy of credit, like those who administer a deadly drug with sweet wine."

> For they speak of Christ, not that they may preach Christ, but that they may reject Christ; and they speak of the law, not that they may establish the law, but that they may proclaim things contrary to it. For they alienate Christ from the Father, and the law from Christ. They also calumniate his being born of the Virgin; they are ashamed of his cross; they deny his passion; and they do not believe his resurrection. They introduce God as a Being unknown; they suppose Christ to be unbegotten; and

as to the Spirit, they do not admit that he exists. Some of them say that the Son is a mere man, and that the Father, Son, and Holy Spirit are but the same person, and that the creation is the work of God, not by Christ, but by some other strange power.[3]

Differences in theology likewise led to differences in church practice, as some followers did not share in the eucharist or the prayers of the gathered faithful.

Amid widespread local interpretations of what it meant to be a follower of Jesus and to live the Christian life, church leaders attempted to come to a common understanding of the "apostolic tradition" that could define true Christian belief and practice. "By appealing directly to the apostles and those taught directly by them as the true standard for authenticity," notes historian Rebecca Lyman, "Christians believed that they possessed the saving practice and belief of Jesus."[4] In the ancient world, just as in the world of higher education today, the trustworthiness of a teacher was linked to knowing who that teacher's teacher had been, so the notion of apostolic succession was the "proof" of true apostolic teaching. Who were these apostles? They were the bishops who led the early communities in Jerusalem, Antioch, and Rome; a direct connection to one of these bishops, therefore, was an important validation of a particular teaching or text. But given the wide-ranging beliefs and teachings of the diverse group of missionaries who preached the gospel throughout the Roman empire, in practice the notion of defining Christian truth by following those teachers who were in a continuous line of apostolic succession was more of an ideal than a reality.

In addition to defining "apostolic," the second-century church also had the much riskier task of deciding what was meant by "tradition." Its theologians and teachers tried to narrow it down by making a distinction between the teachings they considered part of "orthodoxy" (right belief) and those they viewed as heretical (wrong or harmful teachings). These bishops did not have the foundation of a long history of speculative discussions enjoyed by Greek and Jewish philosophers of the time, who through their inquiries could continually discover new aspects of the truth. Instead, orthodox

Christians proclaimed a single, unchanging belief inherited by the apostles from Jesus and passed on from one bishop to another. Irenaeus, the second-century bishop of Lyons, affirmed this body of the apostolic teaching in opposition to error—the gnostic interpreters of the gospel—in a treatise opposing heresy:

> The true *gnosis* [knowledge] is the doctrine of the apostles, and the ancient constitution of the church throughout all the world, and the distinctive character of the body of Christ according to the successions of bishops. . . . And above all, it is the preeminent gift of love which is more precious than knowledge [*gnosis*], more glorious than prophecy, and which excels all other gifts of God.[5]

According to Irenaeus, this "rule of faith" could arguably be found in a Christian community, provided it is authentic and true, and not one established by false teachers. Yet in the same treatise he accuses these "false persons, evil seducers, and hypocrites" of entrapping Christians by imitating orthodox language while teaching deception. For their part gnostic teachers accused the Christians of inhospitality, asking why, even while "they say the same things, and hold the same doctrine," the Christians keep themselves "aloof from their company" and "call them heretics."[6]

One of the difficulties for us as we try to identify these varying doctrines from a distance is that we hear primarily the voices of the "winners": many of the writings that were viewed as heretical were burned or lost, and their proponents sent into exile or silenced. In recent years newly discovered manuscripts such as the Gospel of Thomas and Gospel of Philip have shed interesting light on the diversity of beliefs in the second-century churches. Because Christian communities from their beginnings and throughout these early centuries worshiped primarily in one another's homes, privately and often in secret, they were almost impossible to regulate. Suppressed factions also found refuge in the privacy of supportive households—just as orthodox Christians did during periods of persecution by the Roman authorities. Later we will see Hilary, the orthodox bishop of Poitiers in the mid-fourth century, when the

Arians controlled the basilicas and the supporters of Nicea were out of imperial favor, urging his flock to "follow the example of the early Christians who resisted the decrees and edicts of governors and gathered secretly in households." The private households of ascetics and prophetic leaders whose devotional practices were viewed with doubt by those in authority functioned as "a kind of wild ecclesiastical frontier keeping the careers of outlawed theologians alive and allowing for the survival of diverse Christian practices frowned upon by officials."[7]

In one of Tertullian's second-century treatises against heretical teachings, we see (from his point of view) some of the beliefs that stood in opposition to those espoused by the churches that were considered orthodox:

> I must not leave out a description of the heretics' way of life—futility, earthly, all too human, lacking in gravity, in authority, in discipline, as suits their faith. To begin with, one cannot tell who is a catechumen and who is baptized. They come together, listen together, pray together. Even if any of the heathen arrive, they are quite willing to cast that which is holy to the dogs and their pearls (false ones!) before swine. The destruction of discipline is to them simplicity, and our attention to it they call affectation. They are in communion with everyone everywhere. Differences of theology are of no concern to them as long as they are agreed in attacking the truth. They are all puffed up, they all promise knowledge.

Tertullian goes on to rail against the practices of these heretical communities, which apparently viewed the ordering of ministries in the church and the role of women in leadership rather differently from his own church in Carthage:

> As for the women of the heretics, how forward they are! They have the impudence to teach, to argue, to perform exorcisms, to promise cures, perhaps even to baptize. Their ordinations are hasty, irresponsible, and unstable. Sometimes they appoint novices, sometimes people tied to secular office, sometimes

renegades from us, hoping to bind them by ambition as they cannot bind them by truth. Nowhere can you get quicker promotion than in the camp of the rebels, where your mere presence is a merit. So one man is bishop today, another tomorrow. The deacon of today is tomorrow's reader, the priest of today is tomorrow's layman.[8]

In these and other bitter feuds between Christian communities, we see that the story of the early church is not a story of uniformity, but of varying traditions and practices informed by the cultures and religious background of the local peoples, who were a part of a complex network of diverse communities with distinctive interpretations of the Christian faith and practice. In fact, it seems much like the church we know today.

Clearly, for the first two or three centuries of its life, Christian orthodoxy was maintained by the bishops of the churches, along with the presbyters and deacons who served as local leaders, and while these communities shared beliefs in common with Christians in other locations, there was not a single creed that contained the whole of Christian belief. Even the adage *lex orandi, lex credendi* ("the rule of prayer is the rule of belief," meaning that our experience of God in prayer will inform and shape our theological understandings of God) will not ensure theological uniformity, for as we see in our churches today it is entirely possible to worship alongside people who hold distinctly different interpretations of the liturgy we share. The rule of belief in the second century was not a set creed, as would develop in the centuries to come, but simply a brief summary of the gospel that was part of the baptismal confession of faith in one God who was the creator of all and the Father of Jesus Christ; in Jesus the Christ, who was born of a virgin, who died and was raised from the dead, and who would return in glory; and in the Holy Spirit, who was given in baptism and who would continued to speak through the prophets and community of the faithful. This simple rule of faith allowed for diverse interpretations among the local communities in the early centuries—a diversity that in the fourth century could no longer be tolerated when the church after Constantine was expected to be the source of unification of the empire and the whole political realm.

THE CREED

In many churches today we recite a creedal statement of belief in the midst of our Sunday worship. And yet many of us have had conversations in which our fellow worshipers later confide they "have some problems with the creed." For some the problem is the language of the creed, which seems outdated at best; for others the theology is incomprehensible or even contradictory to what they have come to believe about God. What does it mean, for example, to say Jesus is "true God from true God, begotten, not made, of one Being with the Father"? Can we who have a twenty-first-century understanding of the universe still truly affirm that Jesus "ascended into heaven and is seated at the right hand of the Father"? And what does it mean to believe in "one holy catholic and apostolic Church"?

In a personal essay, theologian Martin Smith wonders what our relationship with the ancient creeds might be today: "Can we love them?" he asks. "Can we have an understanding with them?" As he pondered his own relationship with the creeds, he examined more closely the symbolic nature of the creeds in the early church, remembering that in these early baptismal liturgies new converts would recite the *symbolum apostolorum,* the Apostles' Creed, or "symbol" of the faith. "To me," Smith explains, "there is the encouraging suggestion that the creed is a constellation of metaphors and images all crying out for interpretation." Yet he discovered from the literary critic Northrop Frye an intriguing dimension of symbols in the ancient world. When Frye noted that "originally a symbol was a token or counter, like the stub of a theater ticket which is not the performance but will take us to where the performance is," Smith realized that in the same way, the Christian creeds were

> originally created to summarize for converts what baptism was going to let them into. Reciting the baptismal symbol, they were admitted to the drama. The priest was like a theater usher welcoming them into the arena of Christian worship,

prayer, and practice. Once inside, they would experience for themselves what it means to worship the Creator, to have a relationship with Christ, to experience forgiveness, to have resurrection hope.[9]

Thus it was in the context of baptism that converts to the Christian faith were given the opportunity to affirm their belief in God. The earliest forms of a rule of faith were part of the baptismal rite, and consisted of a threefold affirmation of faith in God as Father, Jesus as the Son of God, and the Holy Spirit as the life of God in the believer. The early church liturgical order known as the *Apostolic Tradition* contains a description of how baptism took place in that community:

> As he who is to be baptized is descending into the water, let him who baptizes him say thus: "Do you believe in God the Father omnipotent?" And let the one being baptized say, "I believe." And the giver, having his hand placed on his head, shall baptize him once. And then he shall say: "Do you believe in Christ Jesus, the Son of God, who was born from the Holy Spirit from the Virgin Mary, and was crucified under Pontius Pilate, and died, and rose again on the third day alive from the dead, and ascended into heaven, and sits on the right hand of the Father, and will come to judge the living and the dead?" And when he has said, "I believe," he shall be baptized again. And he shall say again: "Do you believe in the Holy Spirit and the holy Church and the resurrection of the flesh?" then he who is being baptized shall say, "I believe," and thus he shall be baptized a third time.[10]

Although baptismal rites would have varied according to local customs, we see in this example the formulation of a statement of belief that has many of the elements in what became identified and handed down to us as the Apostles' Creed.

After the middle of the third century and into the fourth, synods and councils were increasingly important vehicles for the handing on of apostolic tradition. With the passing on of the first and second generations came a pressing need for closer definition

of the oral tradition, in the form of written statements of faith
that could establish the limits of authentic teaching. So many
councils were called to deal with thorny theological problems of
the time that one observer complained of the roads criss-crossing
the empire being clogged with processions of travelling bishops!
After Christianity was legalized by Constantine in the early
fourth century and in 392 made the state religion by the emperor
Theodosius, the church was responsible for creating social unity
and conformity throughout the Holy Roman empire. Thus
emperors took on the role of calling theological councils so that
the church communities from different cities and regions could
resolve doctrinal issues that divided them, and then used their
political and legal powers to enforce the decisions reached by the
bishops in council.

Much debate and wrangling went on among the bishops when
they gathered in ecumenical councils, which may well have had
the atmosphere of lively political conventions today. The bishops
represented the passionately held understandings of Christian faith
and practice in each of their regions, so often consensus was difficult if not impossible to achieve. It took over fifty years of intense
debate and power politics, along with the rise and fall of opposing
bishops, before the questions underlying the Nicene Creed were
considered settled. Even then, various interpretations of the language of the creed were held along a broad spectrum of theological
perspectives, just as we know to be true in the church today. As the
late Marianne Micks wisely reminds us,

> No modern person, at least no one other than a literalist, thinks
> that heaven is "up"—so that in the Incarnation God "came
> down from heaven"—any more than they believe that God the
> Father has a left hand and a right hand. It is quite probable that
> no bishop at Nicaea did either. Just because we live in the space
> age, we need not assume that our forebears were all incapable of
> recognizing metaphors when they used them.[11]

Thus creeds were valued not so much for their theological clarity or innovation as for their primary connection to the apostles.

Although these statements of belief are couched in language and images that made sense within the cultures of the bishops and theologians who developed them, the creeds were revered above all because it was believed that they bore witness to the faith once delivered to the saints.

WHO IS JESUS?

The Nicene Creed is perhaps the most familiar statement of belief for Christians of all denominations. The creed as we know it in the Episcopal eucharistic liturgy was agreed upon by the first great ecumenical Council of Nicea in 325, and further developed at the Council of Constantinople in 381. It was introduced into the liturgy first in the eastern churches, and by the eleventh century appears as a regular part of the Roman mass on Sundays and festivals. The Nicene Creed is identified as part of the essential apostolic teaching of the apostles that is "essential to the restoration of unity among the divided branches of Christendom" in the nineteenth-century document known as the Chicago-Lambeth Quadrilateral, and thus is viewed as one of the four fundamental pillars of ecumenical unity (BCP 877). We can affirm that its authority comes directly from the teaching and preaching of the earliest Christian community.

To understand the significance of the Nicene Creed we need to look first at the complex yet fundamental theological questions that were being asked at the time about the man they came to know as Savior and Lord. *Who is Jesus?* This question has been asked by every generation since the first Easter, and is still being asked today. And just as we do, early Christians answered it in multiple ways, according to their cultural assumptions and experiences of God. Jewish Christians who believed that Jesus was more than a prophet, but was sent from God, somehow *was* God, faced the difficult question of how they could confess belief in two gods, and still remain faithful to the revelation of *one* God who was above all the gods of the nations, as taught throughout the Hebrew scriptures. Daily in the temple and in their homes they prayed the *Shema*, "Hear O Israel, the Lord our God, the Lord is One." How could Jesus be God? How did he fit with the God who was known as the Creator, the God of Israel who had entered into a special covenant with the Hebrew people?

A far different question perplexed those Gentile converts to the Christian faith who came from Greek and Roman culture, with its numerous gods and philosophical traditions of Platonism and Stoicism. For them, affirming belief in Jesus as God contradicted something fundamental in their belief about God. For it was an important tenet of Greek and Roman philosophy that God must be beyond all suffering and change; that being so, how could this God die in agony on the cross? And while it was not uncommon in the ancient world to believe in gods who took on human form temporarily, Christians believed the incarnation of God in Jesus was unique—a decisive and singular event in human history like no other.

Different teachers and schools of thought resolved these issues in different ways. Two dominant understandings of the nature of Jesus emerged in the second century and laid the foundations for the controversies of the third and fourth. In the approach known as *adoptionism*, Jesus was seen as a human prophet upon whom the Spirit had descended in baptism, an inspired man who fulfilled the will of God, who suffered, died, and was raised from the dead. Adoptionists believed God had "adopted" Jesus as his "son." This approach had the advantage of preserving Jewish monotheism, for it meant that Jesus was not God and did not share a divine nature with God.

The other approach to the question of who Jesus was in relation to God is called *modalism*. Modalists believed that God was one being, acting according to different "modes" or roles throughout human history, but not three distinct persons existing simultaneously. Historian Rebecca Lyman explains that "one way to understand this theological model is to think of ourselves as one person in three different roles: for example, I am a professor, a mother, and a priest, but always myself, simply performing different functions."[12] Modalism was appealing in that it could affirm the divinity of Jesus while also appearing to preserve the unity of God's nature as one. Yet over time the orthodox theologians rejected it because of Scripture's witness that God exists as Father, Son, and Spirit as separate persons.

Theologians continued to offer variations on these two approaches as the church struggled with how to understand the relation of God and Jesus, and the experience of the Holy Spirit in the church's life and worship. It was a priest from Alexandria named Arius who became the catalyst for the calling of the council at Nicea by accusing his bishop, Alexander, of being a modalist. If God the Father was the creator, Arius reasoned, and the Son was "begotten of the Father," then there must have been a time when the Son did not exist. Therefore Jesus could not share the divine nature of God the Father. Arius's solution addressed the thorny philosophical question of how God the Son could suffer and die on the cross while at the same time preserving the monotheism of the Jewish tradition from which Christianity emerged. Bishop Alexander responded that Arius was teaching adoptionism, and thus denying the divinity of Jesus. The church in Alexandria was deeply divided by the very public argument, with the clergy, women ascetics, and lay people choosing sides and provoking dissension and even violence in the streets of the city. In the face of such irreconcilable positions, both parties appealed for support beyond the diocese, leading to the calling of all the bishops at imperial expense to the summer palace at the resort town of Nicea.

After much argument, wrangling, and compromise, and led by Athanasius, Alexander's successor as bishop of Alexandria, the bishops drafted a creed that affirmed Jesus as the "Son of God" who was "begotten not made, of one substance with the Father" and who "became incarnate." Although all of the bishops were required to affix their signatures to the statement, many did not agree with its teachings and were soundly criticized for assenting to it when they returned to their local churches. One bishop—Leontius, the bishop of Syrian Antioch—even resorted to "mumbling the doxology inaudibly in order to avoid outbreaks of conflict among his sharp-eared and sharply divided congregation," since Arians prayed *to* the Father, *through* the Son, and *in* the Holy Spirit, while the Nicenes prayed *to* all persons of the Trinity equally.[13] The controversy over the nature of Jesus the Son would continue for decades to come. Even after the Council of Constantinople reaffirmed the creed of Nicea and added a paragraph clarifying the nature and work of the Holy Spirit, Arian Christianity flourished and was the predominant tradition in many local churches led by Arian bishops well into the fifth century.

Those of us living some seventeen hundred years later may look incredulously at the vicious quarrelling over theological words or categories of philosophical thought that took place in the fourth and fifth centuries. Gregory of Nyssa complained he could not even do his shopping in the marketplace or go about his daily routine without engaging in theological disputes: "If you ask any one in Constantinople for change, he will start discussing with you whether the Son is begotten or unbegotten. If you ask about the quality of bread, you will get the answer: 'The Father is greater, the Son is less.' If you suggest taking a bath you will be told: 'There was nothing before the Son was created.'"[14] Yet at the heart of these arguments is a question that is pressing in our own day as well: *How do human beings experience salvation in God?* If Jesus was not of the divine nature with God, Athanasius and his fellow orthodox bishops reasoned, then humanity has not been taken up into God, and we are not saved. Unlike the relationship between the Creator and those who are created, fathers and sons *can* share a common nature, Athanasius argued against the Arians, so it was possible that Jesus was indeed fully divine even while fully man: "He became flesh, not that he has been changed into flesh, but that he has taken living flesh on our behalf and has become man." Likewise, Gregory of Nazianzus, the fourth-century Archbishop of Constantinople, would affirm that only a fully human man, united to God, could heal and save humanity: "For that which he has not assumed he has not healed; but that which is united to his Godhead is also saved."[15]

The christological controversies of the second, third, and fourth centuries evolved into and overlapped with disputes about the nature of the Trinity, culminating in the Council of Chalcedon in 451. In some ways the controversies were never completely resolved: the opposing bishops were simply exiled and orthodox bishops put in their place. Over time, the focus for debate shifted to other aspects of the faith, including the practice of spiritual disciplines that led to growth in the Christian life. Many Christians were content to leave the finer points of theological discussion to the realm of mystery and simply to accept the Trinity as the manner in which God has chosen to be revealed. Every century since then, if not every generation of teachers and theologians, has found new ways of talking about and experiencing the mystery of God in all its infinite variety and richness.

In the centuries after Nicea, the regular recitation of the Nicene Creed found its way into the celebration of the eucharist, and the practice continues today in our Episcopal liturgies, after the hearing of Scripture and the preaching of the sermon. For many of us, reciting the creed is a spiritual discipline that is part of the way we reaffirm our baptismal commitment to "continue in the apostles' teaching." One contemporary writer has compared this discipline to re-pounding the nails that work loose in the clapboards of his home in New Hampshire in response to seasonal changes in temperature and the passage of time. "One of the great joys of repeating the traditional creeds of the Christian church," writes Gordon MacDonald, "is that it gives us an opportunity to reaffirm the central truths of God's revelation. As we say, 'I believe . . .' we begin to hammer back the nails of our convictions and commitments."[16]

THE BREAKING OF BREAD AND THE PRAYERS

Just as Christians valued these creeds as essential to the true apostolic tradition, so too during these early centuries the liturgy of the church came to be regarded as part of the same inheritance, perhaps most especially the baptismal and eucharistic rites. The earliest Christians in Jerusalem had continued the Jewish tradition of praying throughout the day at the hours of prayer and gathering for meals in their homes. These meals, which included prayers of thanksgiving and the sharing of bread and wine in remembrance of Jesus, both created and affirmed a sense of unity in a common life of faith. This meal was given a variety of names—the Lord's Supper, the breaking of bread, a love feast (or agape), a memorial, communion, mystery, sacrament—and it took a variety of forms as Christianity spread beyond Jerusalem, and adapted to the Greco-Roman traditions of household life and the sharing of meals. Almost all included the sharing of bread and wine, but we also see in some places the sharing of milk and honey at baptism, and the blessing of cheese and olives at the ordination of a bishop.

In the second-century *Didache*, we see worship taking place in small house churches within the context of a meal in which only the baptized could participate. The prayers were written down, but leaders were allowed to extemporize as well:

> And concerning the Eucharist, hold Eucharist thus: First concerning the Cup, "We give thanks to you, our Father, for the Holy Vine of David your child, which you made known to us through Jesus your child; to you be glory for ever." And concerning the broken Bread: "We give you thanks, our Father, for the life and knowledge which you made known to us through Jesus your child. To you be glory for ever. As this broken bread was scattered upon the mountains, but was brought together and became one, so let your Church be gathered together from the ends of the earth into your Kingdom, for yours is the glory and the power through Jesus Christ for ever." But let none eat or drink of your Eucharist except those who have been baptized in the Lord's name.[17]

Gradually the household sharing of bread and wine as part of a communal meal of Christian unity, celebrated with Scripture readings, prayers, and thanksgivings, was separated from the context of the meal. Liturgical scholars do not know exactly why or when this separation happened; certainly it took place at different times in different places, perhaps in response to edicts that banned club or religious gatherings in the evening, or to the abuses that Paul mentions in his letters to the church in Corinth, in which some members ate greedily while others went hungry. In some communities the context of a fellowship meal survived in some form long after it was lost in other places. In mid-second-century Rome, by the time Justin Martyr wrote his description of how they celebrated the eucharist, all that is left are the rituals surrounding the blessing of bread and wine:

> And on the day called Sunday an assembly is held in one place of all who live in town or country, and the records of the apostles or the writings of the prophets are read for as time allows. Then, when the reader has finished, the president in a discourse admonishes and exhorts (us) to imitate these good things. Then we all stand up together and send up prayers; and as we said before, when we have finished praying, bread and wine and water are brought up, and the president likewise sends up prayers and thanksgivings to the best of his ability, and the people assent, saying the Amen; and the (elements over which) thanks have been given are distributed, and everyone partakes; and they are sent through the deacons to those who are not present. And the wealthy who so desire give what they wish, as each chooses; and what is collected is deposited with the president. He helps orphans and widows, and those who through sickness or any other cause are in need, and those in prison, and strangers sojourning among us; in a word, he takes care of all those who are in need.[18]

As the eucharistic celebration evolved from an evening gathering around a domestic table in a private house to a morning liturgy at the altar in a public basilica, however, its focus also shifted. No longer a substantial meal and time of conversation, it became instead a token distribution of bread and wine. Moreover, the brief prayers and blessings we see in early documents like the *Didache* and Justin's *Apologia* became more formal and elaborate in the glorious setting of imperial churches. Ironically, notes historian Andrew McGowan, "as less was eaten, more and more seems to have been said over the sacral foods."[19] This former connection between the bread and wine of the eucharist and its original context of an extended meal of shared conversation and nourishment enjoyed in the fellowship of the church is still lost for most of us today. Episcopalians who receive a stiff, embossed paper wafer in their hands as they stand in line or kneel uncomfortably at an altar rail may well want to inquire, as one child recently asked her priest at the altar rail, "Is this something I can eat?"

By the fourth century, church leaders who were troubled by the influx of new Christians who were ignorant of the ethical dimensions of their faith began to focus on the holiness of the eucharistic bread and wine itself, and to warn their congregations against coming to communion without repentance and amendment of life. Rather than inspiring their members to more rigorous discipline, however, the practice led to a falling away in the reception of communion, as members feared the dire consequences of eating and drinking "in an unworthy manner." As the church entered the middle ages, moreover, the liturgy became chiefly a drama enacted by the clergy for spectators, and the eucharistic bread a sacred object of devotion rather than food to be shared. It would be a fundamental purpose of the sixteenth-century Anglican Reformation to restore to the people the practice of receiving both the bread and cup of the eucharist.

ANCIENT CHURCH, FUTURE CHURCH

Classical Anglicanism has always had an enduring bond with the preachers and theologians of the patristic period. The apostolic tradition as it evolved in the early church would become the touchstone and guide for later generations, from Richard Hooker, Thomas Cranmer, and the Anglican leaders of the sixteenth-century English Reformation to Edward Pusey, John Keble, and the Tractarians of the nineteenth-century Oxford Movement. In attempting to find an identity for the English church apart from the Church of Rome, notes Rebecca Lyman, Anglicans "went back not only to scripture, but to these earliest centuries of the church. Here the reformers found a model for liturgy in the language of the people, a learned and pastoral theology, and the shared authority of councils."[20] Their efforts to find a way of being the church that allowed for local variations of practice and belief within a common life, furthermore, found echoes in the writings of the church fathers; in the words of Irenaeus, "Our diversity shows our unity." This Anglican comfort with adapting the apostolic and catholic tradition to local cultures and times is articulated in Article 34 on "Traditions of the Church": "It is not necessary that Traditions and Ceremonies be in all places one, or utterly like; for at all times they have been divers, and may be changed according to the diversity of countries, times, and men's manners, so that nothing be ordained against God's Word" (BCP 874).

Indeed, prior to the compilation of the 1549 Book of Common Prayer, a number of liturgical forms were used in Britain, with common liturgies based on the Roman rite that varied both in wording and in rubrical actions. One of the premier theologians of the Anglican Reformation, Richard Hooker, defended the incorporation of many of the elements of these rites in the prayer book against the reforming tendency to see the apostolic church as a "golden age" to be restored intact:

> In tying the church to the orders of the apostles' times, they tie it to a marvellous uncertain rule, unless they require the observation of no orders but only those which are known to be apostolical by the apostles' own writings. But then is not this their rule of such efficiency, that we should use it as a touchstone to try the orders of the Church by for ever? Our end ought always to be the same, our ways and means thereunto not so. The glory of God and the good of His Church was the thing which the apostles aimed at, and therefore ought to be the mark whereat we also level.[21]

Writing in 1936 while he served as a lecturer to ordination candidates in Lincoln, Michael Ramsey, who would later become the 100th Archbishop of Canterbury, likewise emphasized the importance of the church of the first five centuries, "not as a golden age nor as a model for the imitation of Christians . . . , but as an age when the whole gospel found expression in the life and liturgy of the one Body." In these early centuries, Ramsey observed, "the Syrian, the Greek, and the Roman were in one fellowship, with a eucharistic worship exhibiting something like a balance of all the elements of thanksgiving, commemoration, fellowship, sacrifice, mystery."[22] It was its effort to hold this unity of worship within a diversity of church order and teaching that marked the early church as a remarkable era in church life.

Valuing the life of the early church for Anglicans without seeing it as something simply to be duplicated had profound implications for the development of Anglican and Episcopal liturgies, starting with the first Book of Common Prayer and continuing in our own day with the revision of prayer books throughout the Anglican Communion. The archaeological discovery and recovery of the texts and forms of a number of ancient liturgies in the mid-twentieth century profoundly influenced the scholars who revised and supplemented the prayer books and missals of all the liturgical churches during that time, including our own. We owe our rites for baptism and eucharist, especially Eucharistic Prayer D and the Order for Worship in the Evening, to the recovery of these ancient texts; the widespread practice of celebrating the eucharist as the primary service of worship on Sunday mornings, rather than morning prayer, is part of the desire to return to our roots in the ancient church. Thus from their beginnings—imperfectly and with many bitter disputes and violent consequences along the way— Anglicans have attempted to affirm the theology and prayer of the ancient church while at the same time embracing the thought and insights of their time and culture.

How do Anglicans today honor this spiritual tradition of continuing in "the apostles' teaching and fellowship, the breaking of bread, and the prayers"? In their valuing of "diversity in unity," of tradition, flexibility, and adaptation, the Anglican way has important contributions to make and vital principles of polity and practice to offer Christians living in a postmodern world. We aspire to tolerate different points of view and even a certain amount of ambiguity while sharing a belief in a common truth that unites us all living in a global society. Brian McLaren, theologian of the emergent church, writes of seeking after these ancient practices as part of a desire to "capture that fusion of everyday sacredness" that characterized the faith of the early church—the recovery of chanted prayers and silence, the lighting of candles and sharing of bread and wine, the taking on of a rule of life and the practice of hospitality and service.[23] These seekers from emerging churches, liturgical churches, and no church at all are discovering in the Christian faith a way of living spiritually they may have never known before.

Yet liturgist Patrick Malloy would caution those who seek to adopt the "ancient patterns" of the liturgical traditions without wrestling with the truth and purpose of the theologies and creedal beliefs these traditions embody:

> Emergent Christians have unreflectively retained (speaking generally, as one must of everything in emergence) the dominant theology of the tradition from which most of them are emerging. The ancient symbols are reappropriated, but the patristic conviction that the symbols and symbolic actions constitute an objective, efficacious encounter with the Holy is not. These symbols are used because they make an impression. The subjectivism of modernism—that these patterned behaviors "work" for some people—is why they are encouraged. Nothing is said about how they mediate Divine Life. Emergence has not worked out, and even eschews, a theology of symbolic action.[24]

In other words, the practices and creeds and prayers of the ancient church are not self-help techniques to be adopted to make us feel better about ourselves, or more "spiritual," but an essential part of the conversation between belief and prayer, doctrine and practice that comprises the Christian faith and life. "A doctrine-free spirituality risks descending into sentimentality," note the editors of a volume on Anglican theology, and offers but weak support for the spiritual life in the political and cultural world in which we live. Without discipline and doctrine, spirituality will become empty; on the other hand, without the personal experience of holiness in our prayer and liturgical life, doctrine itself "becomes idle, even idolatrous."[25]

It is precisely because our praying and believing are inextricably intertwined that we cannot ignore the real dissonance in language and worldview between the ancient creeds and theological understandings of God in the twenty-first century. And yet, we are reminded, "if some area of doctrinal language has become apparently arid, the question demanding to be asked is not *first* whether it makes sense before some imaginary tribunal of disengaged intellect or contemporary relevance, but what possibilities for Christian life and discipleship it was meant to 'encode' and whether the problem lies in a shrinking of our imagination in respect of this discipleship."[26] In other words, if our creeds no longer make sense as expressions of our faith in God in Christ, then our task is not to dismiss them as irrelevant, but to recommit ourselves to the discipleship that gave rise to the faith the creeds express. In the course of practicing that discipleship, our minds and hearts will be opened to a vision of God that is broad, strong, and imaginative enough to encompass expressions of the ancient faith of the church as it is known afresh in the twenty-first century.

The study of historical traditions of Christian faith and life is an essential part of this expansion of our imagining of what discipleship might look like in the twenty-first century, and how it might inform our identity as followers of Christ. As evangelical theologian Robert Webber concludes:

> The ancient church did not design (a contemporary word) worship to reach people, to educate people, or to heal people. Yet in their worship, which was a prayer of praise and thanksgiving offered to God, people were indeed led into contemplation of God's mighty acts of salvation and stimulated to live a life of participation in the life of God in the life of the world. The point is, of course, that how we pray shapes who we are.[27]

And so it is to the sanctification of life and Christian holiness in the Anglican tradition that we turn next.

ANGLICAN VOICES ON THEOLOGY

> There is in the world no kind of knowledge, whereby any part of truth is seen, but we justly account it precious. . . . To detract from the dignity thereof were to injure even God himself, who being that light which none can approach unto, hath sent out

these lights whereof we are capable, even as so many sparkles resembling the bright fountain from which they rise.

—Richard Hooker, *Of the Laws of Ecclesiastical Polity*
III.8.9 (1594)

Persecution provoked the spirit which it strove to extinguish. Have compromise and liberality succeeded in repressing it? Is this age, in which all opinions are so commonly believed to be indifferently true, less fruitful of party notions and animosities than any previous age? Do men find fewer excuses than formerly, for quarreling with each other, and hating each other? Would it not be more correct to say, that our modern liberalism means permission to men to quarrel with and hate each other as much as they please?

—F. D. Maurice, *The Kingdom of Christ* (1838)

Life must be something more than dilettante speculation. And religion (ought to be if it isn't) a great deal more than mere gratification of the instinct for worship linked with the straight-teaching of irreproachable credos. Religion must be *life made true*; and life is action, growth, development—begun now and ending never. And a life made true cannot confine itself—it must reach out and twine around every pulsing interest within reach of its uplifting tendrils. . . . Let go your purse-strings and begin to *live* your creed.

—Anna Julia Cooper, *A Voice from the South* (1892)

Learning to see the mystery of God's plan, to see it in a way that illuminates the meaning of the world, requires us to develop some habits of mind and heart. The word "habit" comes from the Latin *habitus,* meaning a condition or character; it is a form of the Latin verb *habere*, meaning to have and to hold. So when theology becomes a habit, it becomes part of your character, a fundamental having and holding of who you are. Or we could say that theology "inhabits" you, that God's Word comes to dwell within your heart by the power of the Spirit.

—Mark McIntosh, *Mysteries of Faith* (2000)[28]

What saddens me these days is how many Christians I meet who identify themselves as "heretics"—jokingly if they are still in churches and defiantly if they are not. For some, the issue is that they believe *less* than they think they should about Jesus. . . . The glory they behold in him has more to do with the nature of his being than with the number of his miracles, but they have suffered enough at the hands of other Christians to learn to keep their mouths shut.

For others, the issue is that they believe *more* than Jesus. Having beheld his glory, they find themselves better equipped to recognize God's glory all over the place, including places where Christian doctrine says that it should not be. . . . These heretics not only fear being shunned for their unorthodox narratives; they also fear sharing some of the most powerful things that have ever happened to them with people who may ridicule them.

Given the history of Christians as a people who started out beholding what was beyond belief in the person of Jesus, this strikes me as a lamentable state of affairs, both for those who have learned to see no more than they are supposed to see as well as for those who have excused themselves from traditional churches because they see too little or too much. If it is true that God exceeds all our efforts to contain God, then is it too big a stretch to declare that *dumbfoundedness* is what all Christians have most in common? Or that coming together to confess all that we do not know as we reach out to one another is at least as sacred an activity as declaring what we think we do?

—Barbara Brown Taylor, "Way Beyond Belief:
The Call to Behold" (2006)[29]

QUESTIONS FOR REFLECTION AND DISCUSSION

1. How would you answer the question "Can we love the creeds?" In what ways do the creeds express your beliefs about God? How do they fail to express what you believe to be true? What is missing? How would you restate the creed?

2. How do you practice the baptismal promise to "continue in the apostles' teaching and fellowship, the breaking of bread, and the prayers"? What are the elements of your spiritual practice that are most meaningful to you right now? How has your practice changed over time?

3. In the passage from Barbara Brown Taylor's essay "Way Beyond Belief" quoted immediately before these questions, she wonders if "coming together to confess all that we do not know as we reach out to one another is at least as sacred an activity as declaring what we think we do." Do you agree with her? Why or why not? What do you do with doubts or uncertainties—all that you "do not know"—when it comes to matters of faith?

Chasing Away Devils, Stirring Up Angels

Will you persevere in resisting evil, and, whenever you fall into sin, repent and return to the Lord? (BCP 304)

A great fullness of spiritual comfort and joy in God comes into the hearts of those who recite or devoutly intone the psalms as an act of praise to Jesus Christ. They drop sweetness in men's souls and pour delight into their thoughts and kindle their wills with the fire of love, making them hot and burning within, and beautiful and lovely in Christ's eyes. And those who persevere in their devotion he raises up to the life of meditation and, on many occasions, he exalts them to the melody and celebrations of heaven.

The song of the psalms chases away devils, stirs up angels to help us; it drives out and destroys discontent and resentment in the soul and makes a peace between body and soul; it brings desire of heaven and contempt for earthly things. Indeed, this radiant book is a choice song in God's presence, like a lamp brightening our life, health for a sick heart, honey to a bitter soul, a high mark of honor among spiritual people, a voicing of private virtues, which forces down the proud to humility and makes kings bow in reverence to poor men, nurturing children with gentleness. In the psalms there is such great beauty of meaning and of medicine from the words that this book is called "a garden enclosed," a sealed fountain, a paradise full of apples.[1]

The words of this English mystic from the fourteenth century show us something fundamental about how Anglicans deal with sin, and what calls them to "repent and return to the Lord." Although Richard Rolle is referring specifically here to the recitation of the psalms in the daily prayers of the church, these words speak to us of God's loving-kindness and mercy, which draws our "agitated and tempestuous souls into a fair and peaceful way of life" through the promise of joy. When we repent of the way of life that exiles us from the life of God, we enter the "true life" in which our words are mingled with the praises of the angels, and in which we "experience the delightfulness of this gift of wonderful sweetness"—indeed, a "paradise full of apples" in which all that is broken is restored to wholeness and what was lost is found. Sin and evil are always close at hand, but so is the goodness of life in heaven, waiting for those who accept it.

The Language of Sin

The second question in the Baptismal Covenant explores dimensions of the spiritual life—"discontent and resentment," in the words of Richard Rolle—that are not always a comfortable fit for us today. We trip up on words like "evil" and "sin" and "repentance"; we prefer the language of psychology, in which we speak of healthy self-improvement and spiritual wholeness in a world where anything is possible for those who try. "For the culture at large," Barbara Brown Taylor tells us in her thought-provoking book *Speaking of Sin*, "religious language has been replaced by the language of spirituality, which uses gentler words such as 'stress-reduction,' 'empowerment,' and 'harmony.'" While there is nothing wrong with these words, she wonders whether "they are adequate to describe the darker realms of human experience, where power is a problem, not an asset, and where harmony is a distant memory from a life that ended a long time ago."[2]

Whatever we call these "darker realms of human experience," we do know their reality in our lives. We know what it is to "miss the mark," as in the Hebrew word for sin; we know the feeling of guilt when we injure those we love or act in ways that alienate and offend. We know what the absence of love or goodness or joy feels like, when life seems to have lost all meaning or purpose. One does not have to be in the middle of life to have awakened with Dante and discovered we were in a "dark wood, where the right road was wholly lost and gone." Some of us have been the recipients or perpetrators—or both—of profound human cruelty; others have endured unspeakable tragedy and loss. Depending on how we were raised through childhood, we may have known or witnessed the terror of parental judgment and the pain of punishment. And if our early experience of God has been dominated by a constant awareness of a sense of failure to measure up or to belong, a deep ambivalence about relating to a God of judgment may haunt us as adults and hinder our growth into spiritual maturity.

Throughout history Christians have identified and named this experience of sin in many different and sometimes contradictory ways. Are we "sinners in the hands of an angry God," or the beloved children of a kind and benevolent Father who rushes to meet his prodigals when they return home? Are we born into a state of fallenness so profound that "there is no health in us," or is the image of God in us marred but not so entirely obscured by human failing? Over time, and within each period of their history, Anglicans have found themselves at various points across the theological spectrum of sin and judgment, mercy and redemption, wrath and loving-kindness.

The words of the prayers used in the eucharistic liturgies of the Book of Common Prayer are perhaps one way to see how our sense of our relationship to God has been shaped by changing cultural understandings of human life. Prior to the 1979 revision, the language of the prayers of confession and preparation for receiving God in the bread and wine of communion is largely penitential in tone, keenly aware of our dependence on God for mercy. The prayer known familiarly as the Prayer of Humble Access has been used for centuries, and contains echoes of the words of the Canaanite woman who approaches Jesus asking him to heal her daughter, even if it means accepting that healing as a mere crumb thrown to the dogs under the table (Mark 7:28):

> We do not presume to come to this thy Table, O merciful Lord, trusting in our own righteousness, but in thy manifold and great mercies. We are not worthy so much as to gather up the crumbs under thy Table. (BCP 337)

This prayer was not included in the contemporary eucharistic rite in the 1979 Prayer Book, which simplifies the penitential language and emphasizes the theme of thanksgiving.

Similarly, the earlier version of the prayer of confession, retained only in the Rite I liturgy, reads:

> We acknowledge and bewail our manifold sins and wickedness,
> which we from time to time most grievously have committed,
> by thought, word, and deed, against thy divine Majesty,
> provoking most justly thy wrath and indignation against us.
> We do earnestly repent,
> and are heartily sorry for these our misdoings;
> the remembrance of them is grievous unto us,
> the burden of them is intolerable. (BCP 331)

Compare this to the contemporary version:

> Most merciful God,
> we confess that we have sinned against you
> in thought, word, and deed,
> by what we have done,
> and by what we have left undone.
> We have not loved you with our whole heart;
> we have not loved our neighbors as ourselves.
> We are truly sorry and we humbly repent. (BCP 360)

Episcopalians who grew up learning the older prayers of penitence by heart and kneeling through most of the church service may have a rather different experience of God from those who have known only the 1979 prayer book, with its encouragement to stand in prayer as the beloved community of children who offer praise and thanksgiving to a benevolent Creator and Redeemer. The God of judgment may be too harsh and distant for some; the God of community may be too familiar and subjective for others. The traditional and contemporary rites both have truths to teach about God and about the reality of sin and evil in human life.

However Anglicans have understood the nature of sin and evil over the centuries, most of the Anglican spiritual traditions that help us to deal with these realms of human experience can be gathered under the general and very practical notion of sanctification—that by God's grace we are in the process of being restored to wholeness and holiness of life. Growth in holiness that is not just a collection of self-help techniques for improvement or a happy life, but a deepening identification with and experience of the living God. "Talking about spirituality simply in terms of an undefined intensity or 'authenticity' of human life," the editors to a volume of readings in the Anglican spiritual tradition have noted, "has little to do with talking about holiness, because holiness presupposes a transcendent source and measure for itself. To speak at all about Christian holiness is to seek for the criteria by which a life can be recognized as communicating the holiness of God as made known in Jesus."[3] Thus sanctification is about making human life holy—or becoming truly human. For Anglicans this process of growth in holiness is usually marked by a love of Scripture, participation in the liturgies and sacraments of the church, especially the Holy Eucharist, and the valuing of a life of prayer in community. But as we have seen, it all begins with baptism.

LEARNING REPENTANCE

In asking us to "persevere in resisting evil," the second question of the Baptismal Covenant calls us to the hard but hopeful work of nurturing spiritual growth and knowledge of God in a world that continually challenges the development of such virtues as goodness and love, justice and peace. If our baptism is the place where we start our journey, our sanctification and growth in holiness will "have to be worked out with long-term and dogged perseverance."[4] Our commitment is renewed and tested and worked out in the private and public spheres, in our prayers offered in secret and in the daily decisions and acts that shape our lives. In this process of persevering day by day to overcome the forces that pull us away from the life of God, we rise and fall time and time again. As John McQuiston points out in the title of his modern paraphrase of the sixth-century Rule of St. Benedict, in a life of ongoing conversion "always we begin again." Such an awareness of the need to begin again throughout our lives dispels any mirage of easy upward mobility in the spiritual life, but also gives us strength and courage to persevere in hope, until Christ is indeed the center of our whole life.

This second question echoes the threefold commitment made earlier in the rite by baptismal candidates to "renounce Satan and all the spiritual forces of wickedness that rebel against God." In the early church such renunciations were expressed both verbally and physically, as the candidates turned their whole bodies to face the west, where they believed the devil was symbolically to be found. In some liturgies they were directed to "breathe on him so that you may begin the battle against him." After they spoke the words of renunciation, they then turned to the east, the place of light, and allied themselves to Christ. This process was repeated three times, with the candidates renouncing every aspect of their former life that contradicted their new life in Christ, and adhering to a new Lord and Savior.[5] In this way the spoken renunciation of evil and repeated turning toward the light reflected the inward and spiritual process of what it meant to leave paganism behind and enter the Christian community.

The fourth-century bishop Theodore of Mopsuestia described the renunciations in his instructions to the candidates for baptism in his diocese, telling them that the meaning intended by the affirmation "I renounce Satan" is that "we have nothing in common with him." Through the grace of Christ we are freed from oppression and liberated from slavery. "Now I know my benefactor," we are able to affirm. "I recognize my Savior. For truly my benefactor is my Savior, who created me when I was not, who grants me favors every day, who does not turn away from me even when I rebel." And so in our baptismal renunciation we pledge to avoid the company of Satan, vowing never to seek it again. "I shall have nothing to do with him," we resolve, "for he was the cause of evils without number." This, Theodore concludes, "is the meaning of 'I renounce.'"[6]

For some early Christians this profession of faith would mean a change in their work or professional life; teachers, for example, were often required to instruct pupils about the Roman gods and religious beliefs, while government officials were expected to be loyal to the various cults of worship. Those Christians who refused to worship the Roman gods or the emperor as required by law lost their jobs—or even their lives, martyred at the hands of Roman authorities. Renunciations of paganism were not made lightly. And the cost of discipleship has remained high in times throughout history and to our own day in those places where the political powers are bent on destroying those who affirm their belief in Christ alone. Countless Anglicans over the centuries have given their lives over to death rather than compromise their faith in Christ, from the English reformers of the sixteenth century to bishops James Hannington and Janani Luwum in Uganda to civil rights worker Jonathan Daniels.

Like the modifying of renunciations in the baptismal liturgy, now spoken rather than acted, this experience of turning from one way of life and entering another is less tangible for many Episcopalians today. Many of us grew up in households that practiced some form of Christian faith, so our experience of conversion may be more of an ongoing deepening and discovery of adult faith than a watershed moment of clear and unwavering commitment. And yet one of the most beloved and sustaining dimensions of the Anglican way is its affirmation of the holiness of ordinary life, and the opportunities to love God afforded by the present moment, in whatever circumstances we find ourselves.

Practicing Holiness

Growth in holiness, like physical development, does not just happen; it must be nurtured and tended with intention and care. For most of us, that nurture takes place in community, among those with whom we live and work and worship. When Benedict of Nursia advised his monks how to resist the "zeal of bitterness which separates from God" and to foster the "good zeal which separates from evil and leads to God," he immediately placed that struggle in the context of community life:

> This, then, is the good zeal which members must foster with fervent love: "They should each try to be the first to show respect to the other" (Rom. 12:10), supporting with the greatest patience one another's weaknesses of body or behavior, and earnestly competing in obedience to one another. No monastics are to pursue what they judge better for themselves, but instead, what they judge better for someone else.[7]

In other words, holiness is not learned in isolation but in community, not in abstract theological principles but in showing patience and care for others, and in paying attention. In the words of Joan Chittister, holiness is learned by "caring for the people you live with and loving the people you don't and loving God more than yourself"; we must develop eyes to see and ears to hear, "listening for the voice of God everywhere in life, especially in one another" and here in the present moment.[8]

This aspect of "listening for the voice of God everywhere in life" on the path to holiness has been practiced in myriad ways through the centuries, but one strong characteristic of Anglican spirituality is its focus on the simple, ordinary, "daily" quality of human life lived in the presence and companionship of God, in the fellowship and community of others. We see this focus in the short prayers and blessings that punctuated the days and nights of Celtic Christians in the early centuries of the church in Britain. "I kindle my fire this morning, in the presence of the holy angels of heaven," a mother would pray at the lighting of the morning fire. "God kindle Thou in my heart within, a flame of love to my neighbor." Whether tending fields or herding sheep, walking to town or another place of work, a journey blessing would always be said, recognizing the presence of the One who accompanied them on the path:

I on Thy path O God
Thou God in my steps.
Bless to me, O God
The earth beneath my foot,
Bless to me, O God,
The Path whereon I go.

And when the day's work was done, a bed-blessing would bespeak
the security of the encompassing God:

I lay me down with Thee, O Jesus
And mayest Thou be about my bed,
The oil of Christ be upon my soul,
The Apostles' Creed be above my head.
O Father who wrought me
O Son who bought me
O Spirit who sought me
Let me be Thine.

Like the Anglican spirituality that evolved from it, the Celtic world
was deeply incarnational, the place in which God revealed himself.
"Birth and death, waking and sleeping, and in between all the
working hours of each day," writes Esther de Waal, "are all part of
a life in which the presence of God is known. Living and praying
are inseparable."[9]

That is why one spiritual practice many Anglicans find helpful in their efforts to live a more centered and ordered life in
today's fragmented and chaotic culture is the tradition, learned
from Benedict, of establishing a rule of life as a framework and
guide for spiritual growth. In her book subtitled *A Rule of Life for
the Rest of Us,* spiritual director Margaret Guenther notes that "a
good rule is not a complicated 'how-to' manual, but a sheltering
and sustaining *place.* A refuge—not for hiding or avoidance, but
for gathering strength." Thus a rule of life is not a list of things
to do, like a recipe or an instruction manual, but a framework, a
trellis, a structure, a secure and steady place in which our spiritual
lives find the nourishment they need to deepen their life in God

and to grow in wisdom and wholeness. While there are many different ways of developing a rule of life, with a wealth of riches from which to learn in the church's tradition, a rule should be grounded in real life, practical and useful in the here and now. "Making a rule," Guenther reminds us, "must have something to do with real people trying to get through their days mindfully and fruitfully."[10]

A rule of life can be simple or elaborate, and tends to evolve and adapt over time as one's life circumstances and spiritual needs change. Time set aside monthly or yearly for solitary retreat and rest is often one aspect of a rule, and some people choose to include particular acts of service to others or opportunities for pilgrimage. Regular meetings with a confessor or spiritual director can be an important part of a rule, especially now that the practice of private confession has been lost in many parts of the Episcopal Church. While the General Confession may help us to acknowledge the human failings we share with others and our corporate guilt for societal injustice, there are times in our lives when spiritual growth is hindered by a deep-seated wound or persistent habit that can only be healed and brought to light through particular and specific conversation with a wise companion. The Celtic church in particular cherished the art of *anamchairdeas* or soul-friendship, with several of their early monastic rules addressing the duties of these spiritual guides, and in recent decades the art and practice of spiritual direction has seen a revival in the Episcopal Church.[11]

Thus rules of life may vary widely in their scope and complexity, but daily prayer of some form is an essential part of any rule. Many use the various rites for morning and evening prayers or Compline from the prayer book; others incorporate meditation or contemplation, praying with beads or the labyrinth, into their daily routine. Most include the psalms or other passages from Scripture, and readings from books on spirituality, both classic and modern. With the wealth of resources available today, it can be difficult to know where and how to begin, so a consideration of the ways Christians who have gone before us have practiced a life of ordered daily prayer is a useful guide.

THE HOURS OF PRAYER

As we saw in chapter 2, the earliest followers of Jesus devoted themselves "to the apostles' teaching and fellowship, to the breaking of bread and the prayers." While we do not know what form these prayers took, they were no doubt adapted from the Jewish hours of prayer referred to in Psalm 119: "Seven times a day do I praise you." While the pattern of those hours of prayer and praise of God varied in time and place, by the beginning of the common era at least three times a day all activity ceased so that certain prayers could be said and the mind and heart fixed on God. As Christianity spread throughout the Roman empire, the hours of prayer were fixed by the orderly conduct of the Roman workday:

> In the cities of the Empire, the forum bell rang the beginning of that day at six o'clock each morning (prime or "first" hour); noted the day's progress by striking again at nine o'clock (terce or third hour); sounded the lunch break at noon (sext or sixth hour); called citizens back to work by striking at three o'clock (none or ninth hour); and closed the day's markets by sounding again at six o'clock in the afternoon (vespers or evening hour). Every part of daily life within Roman culture eventually came, to some greater or lesser extent, to be ordered by the ringing of the forum bells, including Jewish prayer and, by natural extension, Christian prayer as well.[12]

Whether these prayers were said alone or with others, they remained the prayers of the community, and were not individualistic in nature but included the "the time-honored and time-polished prayers and recitations of the faith." While every Christian was to observe the prayers, Phyllis Tickle notes, "none was empowered to create them." In this practice of individuals praying the shared texts of the church, we see the interplay of prayer and doctrine, spirituality and theology at work.

These hours of prayer were adapted and elaborated upon by the earliest monastics of the church, the desert fathers and mothers, in third-century Egypt, as they sought to live out the apostle Paul's mandate to "pray without ceasing" (1 Thess. 5:17). They developed a system within their communities in which the praying of offices would be done continuously: when one group of monks would complete an office, another group would be ready to begin the next office. In this way the monks introduced the concept of the hours of prayer as "a continuous cascade of prayer before the throne of God"—a practice that lives on in Anglicanism today, almost twenty centuries later.

> Christians today, wherever they practice the discipline of fixed-hour prayer, frequently find themselves filled with a conscious awareness that they are handing their worship, at its final "Amen," on to other Christians in the next time zone. Like relay runners passing a lighted torch, those who do the work of fixed-hour prayer do create thereby a continuous cascade of praise before the throne of God. To participate in such a regimen with such an awareness is to pray, as did the Desert Fathers, from within the spiritual community of shared texts as well as within the company of innumerable other Christians, unseen but present, who have preceded one across time or who, in time will follow one.[13]

By the fourth century these prayers were well established as communal offices that included the reading of Scripture, teaching of the faith, chanting of psalms and singing of hymns, and offering of prayers for the church and the world. These simple services of prayer and praise, first offered in homes and then in local churches and cathedrals, were further elaborated with monastic practices during the early middle ages, with the most familiar form being the seven daily hours of prayer and one night office: Vigils, Matins or Lauds, and Prime in the early morning hours, Terce, Sext, and None in the hours of the working day (9 a.m., 12 noon, 3 p.m.), Vespers in the evening, and Compline before bed. These hours of prayer, which became known as the daily or divine office, were kept by monastic communities, clergy and laity in parish churches, homes, and places of work, and came to have a profound influence on the daily prayer and spiritual lives of countless medieval Christians.

The most influential monastic rule was that of Benedict of Nursia, whose simple rule for the community of monks at Monte Cassino in the sixth century would become the basis for many others. Aware of the cathedral offices of prayer from the basilicas in Rome, Benedict adapted them for his purposes and called the offices the *Opus Dei*, or work of God, in which all members of the community participated. Responsibility for observing it were shared among the monks, since Benedict's "little rule for beginners" was designed not to be too burdensome or harsh. Thus his framework for the divine office and other aspects of community life provided ample flexibility to make adjustments according to local conditions and the needs of the monks in varying harvest seasons of the year and changing hours of daylight. The call to communal prayer was to take precedence over all other aspects of the life of the community, such as work or study, for "nothing is to be preferred to the Work of God."

Furthermore, the heart of Benedict's office was the recitation of the psalms, to which more time is devoted in the office than any other aspect. The entire Psalter would be recited by the community every week, and Benedict required that his monks commit the words to memory so they would be immediately at hand, continually informing and shaping the thoughts of the monks. "With its night-time vigil and sevenfold punctuation of the day," writes one Benedictine oblate, "the divine office beats at the very heart of the community's life." This ongoing round of prayer and reading of Scripture "provides a balanced framework into which the monks' other occupations are woven."[14]

Pope Gregory the Great evidently learned of Benedict's Rule from a refugee monk of Benedict's monastery at Monte Cassino, which was destroyed by invading Lombards around 577. He adopted it for the Roman church and sent it to England, along with the Roman liturgies for the offices and the celebration of the eucharist, through Augustine, the prior of the Benedictine abbey of St. Andrew's in Rome who became the first Archbishop of Canterbury. Bishops, abbots, and representatives of the Anglo-Saxon church who attended the second Council of Cloveso in 747 decided that from henceforth the English church would use the Roman liturgy instead of the various local or Celtic rites, and the divine office would be comprised of "the seven hours of prayer for the day and the night with the psalmody and chant belonging to them." Thus the monastic communities and clergy of England adopted the Roman daily office with its regular order of hymns, psalms, and prayers; it was this office that would shape the hearts and minds of the English church in the centuries to come, and form the foundation for Anglican rites of prayer.

With the increasing literacy of medieval Christians, furthered by the invention of the printing press, the practice of praying the daily office moved beyond the monasteries and was reclaimed by the laity of the church. By 1100 many prayer books and breviaries were being hand-copied for monastic chapels and parish churches, as well as shorter books of hours for use in personal devotions. Elaborately illustrated and beautifully crafted, these books were also small enough to be carried around and used throughout the day. Highly prized by people of all social classes, they "democratized fixed-hour prayer, making the daily office a fixture of piety— especially among women—in the middle ages." They also provided a way for families and small lay communities to gather for prayer in the home, comments Diana Butler Bass, making "what had become a clericalized form of prayer their own once again, reclaiming for themselves an ancient practice of the church."[15]

When Thomas Cranmer was compiling the first Anglican Book of Common Prayer in 1549, he consolidated the seven monastic offices into two, "An Ordre for Mattyns dayly through the yere" and "An Ordre for Evensong throughout the yere." These offices are called Morning and Evening Prayer in our 1979 prayer book, which also includes the restoration of an office for noonday (from the "Little Hours" of Terce, Sext, and None) as well as the night office of Compline. We also have available to us a variation of the ancient evening cathedral office, called An Order for Worship in the Evening, with the lighting of the evening lamp as the central element of the service.

The offices Cranmer created have been prayed daily by Anglicans throughout the world, and they became the foundations of Anglican church life until well into the twentieth century.

Whether they were said simply by a few of the faithful gathered daily in quiet parish churches or were celebrated as the primary Sunday morning service or festive evensong complete with men and boys choir, the prayers and praises of the *Opus Dei* have profoundly shaped the Anglican way of Christian living. Some of the prayers for morning and evening are beloved by Anglicans who have repeated them daily throughout their lives, and they speak of the beauty and grace of living an ordered life of faith, as well as the challenges of persevering day after day in resisting all that draws us away from God.

In addition to prayers, the reading of Scripture, and sermons, the daily office has engendered a rich musical heritage in Anglicanism, with settings for the canticles, such as the *Magnificat* and the *Nunc dimittis* sung at evensong, composed by such outstanding musicians as William Byrd, Charles Villiers Stanford, Orlando Gibbons, Herbert Howells, and John Rutter. Settings for the chanting of the psalms are also integral to the service, from medieval plainsong to elaborate choral arrangements, and metrical versions also encourage congregations to participate in singing the canticles and psalms, as well as the hymns.

The forms and texts for the daily hours of prayer have changed and evolved again and again from the gatherings of the earliest disciples to the church of the present day, but they have remained a distinctive and formative aspect of Christian devotion, shaping the minds and hearts of believers in their homes and places of work on a daily basis. They continue to be the common prayer of the church in which praise to God is offered continuously by the people of God—"an act of offering," says Phyllis Tickle, "by the creature to the Creator. The fact that the creature grows strong and his or her faith more sinewy and efficacious as a result of keeping the hours is a by-product (albeit a desirable one) of that practice and not its purpose."[16] In this way the divine office—however and wherever it is prayed—is part of the work of sanctification, of growing in holiness as we become more like the Holy One to whom we offer our praise and thanksgiving through the shared prayers of the Christian community.

TOWARD A HOLY LIFE

One of the great gifts of the Anglican Reformation is the renewed conviction that all of life is holy, and all human beings, no matter what their profession, job, or role in society, are called to participate fully in the life of God. For Anglicans then and now we acknowledge a "priesthood of all believers" in which all are called to holiness of life, rather than only members of the clergy or religious orders. In such a society all are called to become "the 'religious community' in which Gospel imperatives are carried out. Everyone is under monastic discipline, you might say; there is no vicarious holiness."[17]

One aspect of this recognition that holiness of life is not reserved for the saints or clergy or monks of the church has to do with the practice of prayer. For many sixteenth-century Christians, the set prayers and liturgical rites of the church had become too distant, too rote, too identified with the ecclesiastical structures they viewed as corrupt and in need of reform. "Prayer is a lifting up of the mind unto God, or a friendly talking with the Lord, from an high and a kindled affection of the heart," wrote Edwin Sandys, a bishop during the reign of Elizabeth and one of the translators of the Bishops' Bible. We pray directly to God, he affirmed, without need of the intercessions of saints or priestly mediation. How do we pray? "From the heart, 'lifting up pure and clean hands'; that is to say, in faith, and in love. Our prayer, feathered with these two wings, flieth straight into heaven."[18] Several decades later the well-known Puritan fellow of Christ's College, Cambridge, William Perkins, would likewise extol the value of extemporaneous prayer from the heart, urging his students to "pray continually, I mean not by solemn and set prayer, but by secret and inward ejaculations of the heart."[19]

Other leaders in the Elizabethan church sought to reconcile the reforming and catholic traditions that struggled to coexist in the English churches. Thomas Becon, who was a sixteenth-century teacher, priest, and chaplain to Archbishop Cranmer and who was sent to the Tower for a time because of his Protestant beliefs, was a prolific writer on the practice of the Christian life. In his treatise on prayer, he describes the Protestant concern for authenticity in prayer by Christians who live and work in the world and who desire to "pray without ceasing," and yet he also defends the value of the set hours and offices of prayer for all, based on his reading of Scripture:

> Some say that to pray always and not to cease is, throughout all our life fervently to desire that high goodness which is promised us in the world to come. After this sort, say they, whatsoever men do in this life, whether they eat, drink, sleep, work, talk, bargain, study, meditate, etc. so long as this celestial desire remain in them, all their whole life is a certain perpetual prayer. "The perpetual study of living godly," saith Erasmus, "is a continual prayer." . . .
>
> Others affirm that to pray without ceasing is, fervently and with an ardent mind to pray at certain hours destinated and appointed unto prayer. Verily all these expositions, inasmuch as they be godly, are not to be rejected nor cast away. . . . We ought to prescribe and appoint unto ourselves certain peculiar hours every day, which should not pass away without prayer, and which should have the whole affects of the mind utterly occupied in this behalf. . . . And because no man should be offended with the observance and appointment of certain hours unto prayer, as a thing superstitious and repugnant to the christian liberty, I will shew that divers holy men had their certain hours also, wherein they used customably to pray.[20]

Becon then goes on to describe the "seven times in a day" that David prayed and gave thanks to God, including morning, noon, evening, and night, and concludes that these occasions for prayer would "all be very convenient times for a christian man to pray." Here we see the signs of the Anglican efforts to find a "middle way" of cherishing the ancient and catholic traditions of the church while also upholding the Reformation values of locating those traditions in Scripture and aligning one's heart, mind, and soul with the words one prays.

While these early Anglicans might disagree on how and when prayers were to be prayed, those on both ends of the Protestant-Catholic spectrum and everywhere in between would agree that the purpose of prayer was not the earning of grace or the avoidance of divine wrath, but the sanctification of life and growth in holiness. For Anglicans this tends to happen through a deepening congruence between one's beliefs and actions, ongoing repentance and renewal in humility, and a growing identification with the life of Christ through the practice of loving God and neighbor.

A classic Anglican text on these matters is Jeremy Taylor's *Rules and Exercises for Holy Living*. A priest of the High Church party and chaplain to King Charles I until the execution of the king in 1649, Taylor was imprisoned at least twice by the Cromwell government. After the restoration of Charles II, he was named to the see of Down and Connor in Ireland, but remained deeply troubled that he was unable to resolve his many conflicts with the Presbyterian party there. His writings convey the qualities of classic Anglican spirituality characterized by a well-ordered and thoughtful piety that values sober moderation and respect for duty, and is balanced, tempered, and enlivened by an abiding love for God and humankind, and indeed for all creation.

In the first chapter of *Holy Living*, for example, Taylor offers a series of "helps towards a holy life." He begins with advice on the "care of our time" and how to use our "short time here on earth" to good purpose, which is not just for ourselves alone but for the good of society:

> We must remember that we have a great work to do, many enemies to conquer, many evils to prevent, much danger to encounter, many difficulties to be mastered, many needs to serve and much good to do. There are many children to provide for, many friends to support, many poor to relieve, many diseases to cure—besides the needs of nature and family. These private and public responsibilities God has incorporated into the legitimate concerns of religion.

Taylor then provides a list of twenty-three exercises a Christian can do to practice this care of time, from suggesting that "it is good to utter a short prayer or to offer thanksgiving every hour" and to set aside a period of retreat time each year, to offering guidance for the care and nurture of children and the provision of education, to giving practical advice on not "going from house to house" as "tattlers and busybodies," which he warns "is the cancer and rust of idleness." In an exercise that offers hope for many of us living at modern society's frantic pace, Taylor advises, "As much as possible, cut off all useless activities of your life—unnecessary and impractical visits, too much attention to great personalities where neither duty, necessity nor charity obliges you, meetings of no value, or whatever uses up much time to no real civil, religious or charitable purpose."

Next Taylor turns to the "purity of intention," for if we direct our activities "to the glory of God" and intend them for his service, "every action of nature becomes religious and every meal is an act of worship." This sanctification of every dimension of human life is the result of the grace of God, who "makes our very mundane works capable of becoming virtuous, so that in our entire life we may serve Him."

> This grace sanctifies the most common action of our life, and yet without it, the very best actions of our devotion are imperfect and lacking in virtue. He who prays out of habit, or gives alms for praise, or fasts to be considered religious, is but a Pharisee in his devotion, a beggar in his alms, and a hypocrite in his fast. A holy intention sanctifies these and all other actions that can be made holy, and makes them acceptable.

Taylor also recognizes the possibility that our hearts can deceive us when we attempt to discern "whether our intentions are pure and our purposes holy," so he provides a list of signs that provide guidance in judgment. "It is probable that our hearts are right with God and our intentions innocent if we begin our actions with an affection proper to the quality of the work," he begins, "zealous, active," and taking pleasure in religious activities. "But he who does his recreation or his business cheerfully, promptly, and readily, and his spiritual duties slowly, flatly, and without appetite, whose spirit moves like Pharaoh's chariots with the wheels off, it is a sign that his heart is not right with God, but cleaves too much to the world."

Finally, Taylor addresses the spiritual tool of practicing the presence of God in all times and places. God is present everywhere and in everything: "We may imagine God to be as the air and the sea, with all of us enclosed in His embrace, wrapped up in the lap of His infinite nature; or as infants in the wombs of their pregnant mothers. We can no more be removed from the presence of God than from our being."

In these exercises Taylor urges us to "let everything you see suggest to your spirit the presence, excellence and power of God. Let your relationship with creatures lead you to the Creator." He upholds the importance of daily prayer in increasing our awareness of the presence of God, prayer that is offered throughout the day and night in all times and places: "Think of every place as a church," Taylor advises. Further, the presence of God is realized in our care for one another: "God is in the heart of your brother. Refresh him when he needs it, and you give your alms in the presence of God and to God. God feels the relief which you provide for your brother." The result of this exercise is "humility of spirit," he concludes, which "produces an admiration of God's unspeakable mercies and is a source of great modesty in our actions." It also leads to perseverance, for "if we walk with God in all His ways as He walks with us in all ours, we shall be able to keep that rule of God which says, 'Rejoice in the Lord always; and again I say, Rejoice.' St Athanasius once said, 'There is one way to overcome our spiritual enemies: spiritual mirth and perpetually bearing God in our minds.' This effectively resists the devil and allows us to receive no hurt from him."[21]

A close contemporary of Jeremy Taylor, Thomas Traherne, also conveys in his writings the Anglican sensitivity to a world infused with the presence of God, particularly in nature. The seventeenth-century manuscript of his prose-poem *Centuries of Meditation* was discovered by accident by a bookseller in 1896, and today his pleasure in God's creation as a wondrous gift and miracle of life resonates deeply with all who have come to a new appreciation of the earth's beauty and peril in recent decades. Traherne goes beyond simply affirming the wonder of the creation, however; he sees the enjoyment of nature as a spiritual discipline, a way of experiencing

God that is profoundly incarnational in that we are able to see God revealed in even the smallest grain of sand:

> You never enjoy the world aright, till you see how a sand exhibiteth the wisdom and power of God: And prize in everything the service which they do you, by manifesting His glory and goodness to your Soul. . . . Your enjoyment of the world is never right, till every morning you awake in Heaven; see yourself in your Father's Palace; and look upon the skies, the earth, and the air as Celestial Joys: having such a reverend esteem of all, as if you were among the Angels. . . . You never enjoy the world aright, till the Sea itself floweth in your veins, till you are clothed with the heavens, and crowned with the stars: and perceive yourself to be the sole heir of the whole world, and more than so, because men are in it who are every one sole heirs as well as you. Till you can sing and rejoice and delight in God, as misers do in gold, and Kings in sceptres, you never enjoy the world.[22]

Traherne's vision of the God who creates, indwells, and gives life to all things and yet is distinct from them echoes one of the revelations of the fourteenth-century mystic and anchorite Julian of Norwich, in which she was "showed a little thing, the size of an hazel-nut," and marveled when she was told that "it is all that is made." Julian came to understand that "God made it, God loves it, and God keeps it," and thus observed that until she was "in essence one-ed to this Maker, Lover, and Keeper," she would "never have full rest nor true joy." And yet, she maintained, "it is necessary for us to have awareness of the littleness of created things and to set at naught everything that is created, or order to love and have God who is created. . . . His goodness fills all His creatures and all His blessed works, and surpasses them without end, for He is the endlessness."[23]

The ancient Celtic sensibility of the unity of the spiritual and natural realms has similarly influenced Anglican spirituality through the centuries, especially in recent decades as we have come to an appreciation of the earth as a fragile gift from a loving

Creator and ourselves as an interdependent part of that creation. "The Celtic tradition is the ancient or elemental—a return to the elements, the earth, stone, fire, water, the ebb and flow of tides and seasons, the pattern of the year" as the days grow shorter in winter and lengthen in summer, writes Esther de Waal. "To pray the Celtic way means above all to be aware of this rhythm of dark and light. The dark and the light are themselves symbols of the Celtic refusal to deny darkness, pain, suffering and yet to exult in rejoicing, celebration in the fullness and goodness of life."[24] Author and Episcopal priest Nancy Roth expresses a similar blending of concern for the creation and faith in the God who created all that is:

> The word "ecology" is rooted in the Greek *oikos,* a dwelling-place or home. One way to describe the goal of the human journey through life is as a search for at-home-ness: with ourselves, with other people, and with God. Our itinerary leads us to the dwelling-place God gave us, our planet earth. As we learn to love that home, we will increasingly wish to contribute to the earth's preservation and beauty rather than to despoil it. . . . The task will be full of urgency, and also full of joy, for the earth is full of the beauty of holiness, one of the revelations of God.[25]

In these few examples we see some of the ways Anglicans have woven together Celtic, patristic, Benedictine, medieval, and Reformation spiritual themes with a particular view toward the sanctification of all life as the place of revelation of the incarnate God.

LIVING IN THE PRESENCE

Whether through praying the offices throughout the day and night in a "cascade of prayer" shared with countless others or offering family blessings on our daily work and journeys, Anglicans take seriously the need to live in awareness of the presence of God and thus to "pray without ceasing." Many place a high value on the ordering of their days, their work and family life, their relationships with others, and their prayer and worship so as to allow the process of sanctification to proceed unhindered by the distractions of wasted time and busyness that leads only to fatigue and confusion. Most see their participation in the Sunday eucharist as an important part of their worship of God, and have some form of regular daily spiritual practice that includes prayer, silence, and reading. To that end, they often design and stick to an informal rule of life to help guide them along the way.

The ways that Anglicans have sought to live out the baptismal call of continual and ongoing conversion, of living more and more the new and abundant life of which Jesus spoke, vary so considerably they may almost seem too dissimilar to be of the same tradition. But it is important to keep in mind that the Anglican Church was formed as a distinctive "church of the middle way" at the Reformation, one in which Catholic and Protestant sensibilities struggled to coexist side by side. Over time those of Puritan and High Church, Evangelical and Anglo-Catholic, liberal and conservative persuasions have all had a place at the table—and at our best moments, with generosity and grace.

The willingness to live at peace with differences of practice and theology and to have a healthy humility about dictating the religious convictions of others is a hard-won characteristic of Anglicanism that may be especially instructive in today's conflicted world. We need to pay attention to how this willingness gave our Anglican ancestors "a way of talking about God and about the Christian life that was not confined to those who shared their particular theological concerns within the controversies of their day." This conversation could take place then—and perhaps would be made less acrimonious today—by the practice of doing "theology less by the systematic examining of doctrinal structures than by reflecting on the shape of Christian life."[26]

Yet this integration of theology and spiritual practice should not be misinterpreted as a lack of concern for doctrine—which is a common yet mistaken impression often held by those who see the Episcopal Church as "soft" on theology or "wishy-washy" in what it believes. Core beliefs and doctrines *do* inform and shape both our prayer and our practice of the Christian life, as we "continue in the apostles' teaching and fellowship, the breaking of bread and the prayers" while also being attentive to the need for continual repentance, returning, and renewal in our daily lives. For many Anglicans who have gone before us, theology—thinking about God—could never be separated from sanctification—seeking after God while living a life of personal holiness. And if we could begin our conversations today with the common language of living holy lives, rather than focusing on statements of doctrine, we might learn much-needed tolerance and humility in our debates, recognizing that those with whom we disagree aspire to the same holiness of life that we do.

So we turn now to the language and learning that form the backdrop and inform the content of the conversations Christians have about their faith, in their proclamation of the gospel through word and action.

ANGLICAN VOICES ON SANCTIFICATION

> An error groweth, when men in heaviness of spirit suppose they lack faith, because they find not the sugared joy and delight which indeed doth accompany faith. . . . Better it is sometimes to go down into the pit with him, who, beholding darkness, and bewailing the loss of inward joy and consolation, crieth from the bottom of the lowest hell, "My God, my God, why hast thou forsaken me?" (Psal. xxii.1) than continually to walk arm in arm with angels, to sit as it were in Abraham's bosom, and to have no thought, no cogitation, but "I thank my God it is not with me as it is with other men" (Luke xviii.11). No, God will have them that shall walk in light to feel now and then what it is to sit in the shadow of death. A grieved spirit therefore is no argument of a faithless mind.
>
> —Richard Hooker, Sermon I, "Of the Certainty and Perpetuity of Faith in the Elect" (1612)

> Repentance itself is nothing else but a kind of circling; to return to him by repentance, from whom by sin we have turned away. This circle consists of two things. These two things need to be in two different movements. One is done with the whole heart,

while the other is broken and torn. So both things cannot happen at the same time.

First of all you must turn. In this you look forward to God and with your whole heart resolve to turn to him. Then, you must turn again, and this time you look backwards to your sins, in which we have turned away from God. As we look at them our actual heart breaks. One turn is conversion from sin, and the other turn is contrition for sin. One resolves to amend what is to come while the other reflects on and is sorrowful over the past. One resists future evil while the other passes sentence on itself for the evil that it has already done. Between them, these two make up complete repentance, or a perfect revolution.

—Lancelot Andrewes, Sermon Four on Repentance:
Ash Wednesday (1619)

Now, first, you have, you know, the "root of the matter"—and as long as you cling to that, you *can't* go far wrong. As your favourite St. Augustine said, "Love and do what you like!" If you like wrong things, you will soon find the quality of your love affected. . . . It seems to me that your immediate job must be to make this love active and operative right through your life—to live in the light of it all the while, and act by it all the while—to make it light up your relations with other people, with nature, with life, with your work, just as much as it lights up immediate communion with Our Lord. Try to see people by His light. *Then* they become "real." . . . Your attitude towards sin is really almost Calvinistic!! Don't dwell on it! Turn your back on it. Every minute you are thinking of evil, you might have been thinking of good instead. Refuse to pander to a morbid interest in your own misdeeds. Pick yourself up, be sorry, shake yourself, and go on again.

—A letter to a friend from Evelyn Underhill
(January 16, 1908)[27]

It is hope that brings about the change of heart and mind which effects a new orientation in a person's life. . . . To insist on hope as the mainspring of *metanoia* does not, as we have seen, ignore the fact of human evil, of man's perversity and blindness, his arrogance, cruelty and sloth and his timid refusal to respond to summons to change. But psychology makes for a merciful view of human sin, and without condoning wrong-doing makes it possible to feel compassion for the sinner and to hope that divine mercy will heal and forgive him as we pray that our sin may be forgiven and healed.

—Christopher Rex Bryant, SSJE, *The River Within:*
The Search for God in Depth (1978)

The discipline of a rule and vows or promises means simply that I remain a disciple, *discipulus*, one who is a learner, a follower, all my life. The way that Benedict is showing me can never become a closed system. It is more like a series of open doors than a series of prescribed actions.

—Esther de Waal, *A Life-Giving Way: A Commentary on*
the Rule of St. Benedict (1995)[28]

Practicing resurrection means living in openness. It's a vulnerable attitude. Jesus invites Thomas to examine his wounds—come and see the ugliest thing you can imagine. God has made it a source of beauty and healing. It means that our fears, our inadequacies, the wretched parts of ourselves, can be the vehicle for new and more abundant life—if we're willing to confront them honestly and openly. . . .

Practice resurrection. Live in open expectation of the new thing God is doing at all times and in all places. It means opening ourselves to that new thing, recognizing that the change it brings will cause some distress. But there is always more abundant life on the other side of the pain and grief that comes with change and growth.

—Katharine Jefferts Schori, *A Wing and a Prayer* (2007)[29]

QUESTIONS FOR REFLECTION AND DISCUSSION

1. Over the centuries the church has used words such as "sin" and "evil" to describe a sense of alienation from God, or the absence of goodness. What words would you use? How do you make sense of these realities in your own life and the lives of others?

2. What spiritual practices or exercises help you in the process of repenting and returning to the Lord? How have these practices changed over time? Who do you turn to when you need to speak words of confession and truth?

3. In her commentary on the Rule of St. Benedict, Esther de Waal notes that "the way of Benedict is one of continuing and ongoing conversion, of growth and inner transformation, which will go on as long as I live." She then asks herself each day: "Am I being changed by the power of the Gospel? Am I being changed by the presence of God in my life?" How would you answer these questions now? How do you experience "ongoing conversion" in your life? How are you being changed by God and growing in grace each day? What spiritual practices support and sustain your growth in holiness?

Learning Wisdom, Preaching the Word

Will you proclaim by word and example the Good News of God in Christ? (BCP 305)

In 1860, as the American states prepared for war over the right to maintain the biblically sanctioned institution of slavery and Charles Darwin published his research on the origins of human life, the young king and queen of the Hawaiian islands were wrestling with their own questions of faith and the social order. The Congregationalist missionaries who had converted many islanders during the previous decades had established the only church officially recognized in the islands, and the new monarchs were troubled, one Anglican missionary later recalled, by "the comparative dreariness and heaviness of their services." Many of their people were attracted to the Church of Rome "by the greater relief to ear and eye afforded by the services of that Mission," and after much consideration and discussion Kamehameha IV and Emma decided on the Church of England, since it had both the Catholic liturgy they enjoyed and the Protestant beliefs and sensibilities they had embraced. So they sent their request to the British government, and two years later the Right Reverend Thomas Nettleship Staley was dispatched to the islands.

But just before his arrival, tragedy struck the young couple. Their beloved and only son, aged four, suddenly died. Bishop Staley and his wife cared tenderly for the bereaved parents, and during this time the king became a "true and earnest" Christian.

In coping with his grief he devoted himself to his royal duties and even began a Hawaiian translation of the English Book of Common Prayer for his people, but the profound loss cast "a tinge of sadness" on his life that would remain throughout his days.

Not long after his son's death, the king attended a little Congregationalist meeting-house. The native preacher there "preached a strong Calvinist sermon," the Anglican missionary tactfully reported, "in which his zeal outran his discretion, and, no doubt, involuntarily caricaturing the doctrines of his teachers, he descanted at large upon the subject of eternal punishment, apparently losing sight of the general drift of the Bible, and of the aspect in which our Father in heaven is there presented to us." Distressed that his people were being taught "no better ideas of the truth than this," the king announced that he himself would hold another service later that day. Donning a preacher's white surplice, the king mounted the pulpit in the crowded chapel, and preached a very different sermon, choosing for his text only two words: "Jesus wept." Rather than terrifying his people into holiness of life, the king spoke out of his own experience of grief about the comfort of the abiding love of God, a love that gives us true hope and "an incentive to goodness." His sermon was heard and remembered by his people with awe and reverence, especially since it would be one of his last addresses to them. That evening the king had the first attack of the disease that a few months later, at the end of November 1863, "released him from a life which had become very weary to him."[1]

The king intuitively understood the truth of the words historian of preaching O. C. Edwards would write a century and a half later: "There is no activity more characteristic of the church than preaching."[2] While the church has a body of writings that define and describe its doctrines and practices, it is the sermon that interprets and applies and brings alive those beliefs in the lives of the people who are listening. "Sermons are dangerous things," George Herbert wrote in the early seventeenth-century English countryside. Because the words of the preacher have the power to change us, "none goes out of church as he came in, but either better or worse."[3]

What is this power of the word to move and transform, teach and inform? While many of the Protestant reformers marched under the banner of *sola scriptura* and jettisoned many of the traditions of the previous fifteen hundred years in an effort to return to a simpler apostolic faith, the Anglican position was characteristically nuanced, finding a middle way through the extremes that honored both the primacy of the Bible and the value of reasoned interpretation of the truths of the Bible by the people. "The church is our academy," the poet priest John Donne preached to his people. And as with any course of study, he admonished them, members of a congregation can attend services and "yet learn nothing." We must not only show up in church, we must also use the "means"—the tools—provided for learning. "The most powerful means is the Scripture," Donne contended, but mediated through the church, for there the Scriptures are "sealed to thee in the Sacraments and delivered to thee in preaching." While Donne agreed with the reformers that no Christian should be "discouraged from reading the Scripture at home," since in the context of private devotions and study "the Holy Ghost is with thee in the reading of the Scriptures," he urged his congregation to "first learn at church and then meditate at home. Receive the seed by hearing the Scriptures interpreted here and water it by returning to those places at home."[4]

In this chapter we will consider some of the many and varied ways that Anglicans have incorporated "the word" into their spiritual practice, from studying the texts of the Bible and hearing the word preached in sermons to praying prayers and singing hymns so beloved and familiar they are committed to memory. The Anglican literary tradition is rich and vibrant, and includes not only sermons and prayer books but also letters and poems, hymn texts and histories.

"DIVERS TRANSLATIONS"

Just as nations made up of people who speak a variety of languages may be united in their knowledge of the "one God in the unity of faith," wrote Miles Coverdale in the prologue to his first English translation of the Bible, so also are Christians capable of understanding "divers translations" of the Bible despite the fact that they may use "sundry"—or different—words. Coverdale rejoiced that God had "opened unto his church the gift of interpretation and of printing, and that there are now at this time so many, which with such diligence and faithfulness interpret the scripture, to the honour of God and edifying of his people." While some Anglicans were unnerved by the differences in text and interpretation, Coverdale viewed the variety of translations as a benefit to all, comparing the competing translators to a group of archers, each of whom attempts to be closest to the mark and thus spur one another on to their best performance. "Who is now then so unreasonable, so despiteful, or envious," he asks, "as to abhor him that doth all his diligence to hit the prick, and to shoot nighest it, though he miss and come not nighest the mark? Ought not such one rather to be commended, and to be helped forward, that he may exercise himself the more therein?"[5]

Coverdale's work, along with that of other translators such as William Tyndale, was indeed commended: in 1538 Thomas Cromwell ordered in the name of Henry VIII that "one book of the whole Bible of the largest volume in English" be "set up in some convenient place" in the parish church in order to give the people access to the "very lively Word of God,"[6] and the incomparable Coverdale Psalter has been included in almost every version of the Book of Common Prayer since 1549, including our own.

The Reformation's flurry of translations of the Bible into the spoken languages of lay Christians utterly transformed their relationship with Scripture. Not only were the words more easily understood, but also in the age of the printing press Bibles could be purchased relatively inexpensively and used at home in private devotions and study. The Bible has always been central to the Christian faith, studied by theologians and scholars, and known to all through the prayers and hymns of the liturgy, but the printing press brought the words of the Bible into the lives of individuals as never before. As the historian Diarmaid MacCulloch has observed, "Previously, congregations in the West as in the East would have experienced the Bible primarily as performance: countless fragments of it rearranged mosaic-like in the liturgy, mediated through the words of a preacher."[7]

However, now that the Bible could be read like any other book, Christians began to question many of the traditional interpretations, doctrines, and practices that they could not find in these freshly rediscovered scriptural texts, such as the existence of purgatory and the purchase of indulgences. And with the translation and printing of a wealth of ancient theological treatises, scriptural commentaries, and liturgical texts previously tucked away in cathedral or monastic libraries, they were able to understand and embrace in new ways the apostolic faith of the early church and the traditions of eastern Christians. Like the earlier Carolingian renaissance under Charlemagne, the decades leading to the English Reformation were a time of intense learning, exploration, and discovery; increasing literacy made this late medieval literary renaissance more widespread than ever before.

The orderly reading of Scripture had always been a primary focus of the daily office from the early church through the middle ages, and it remained so in the English Reformation church. In his preface to the first Book of Common Prayer, Thomas Cranmer reaffirmed the importance of reading Scripture daily, noting that in earlier times the readings had been so ordered that "the whole Bible (or the greatest part thereof) should be read over once in the year." Through reading and meditating on God's word, Cranmer believed, the clergy and people should "be stirred up to godliness" and "by daily hearing of holy scripture read in the Church should continually profit more and more in the knowledge of God, and be the more inflamed with the love of his true religion." Over time, however, the addition of "uncertain stories, legends," and other extraneous material and "vain repetitions" had broken the pattern and interrupted the reading of a certain book of the Bible, so that in some cases it was begun but never finished. Furthermore, Cranmer lamented, the lessons and prayers were read in Latin, so that although the people heard with their ears, their souls were not edified. Cranmer's solution was to remove many of the Latin "anthems, responses, invitatories, and such like things, as did break the continual course of the reading" and to simplify the calendar of readings so that the lessons for each day would be "plain" and easy to understand.

Cranmer's monumental effort in 1549 to restore the ancient practice of reading through the books of the Bible in the context of daily prayer took root in the English church and eventually bore fruit. The Puritan and Evangelical wings of the English church embraced this study of the Bible wholeheartedly, and those whose piety was more Catholic also continued the practice of incorporating Scripture into their daily devotions, though immeasurably strengthened by the availability of the Bible in English translations.

By 1655, for example, Bishop Jeremy Taylor could assume his readers had access to an English Bible at home, and could use it in their daily prayer and study: "When you are dressed," he advised, "retire yourself to your Closet; and go to your usual devotions." These devotions would include prayers of adoration and thanksgiving, intercession and confession, and "serious, deliberate, useful reading of the holy Scriptures." Taylor then offered five recommendations for this reading:

1. Let it be not of the whole Bible in order, but for your devotion use the New Testament, and such portions of the Old as contain the Precepts of holy life.

2. The Historical and less useful part, let it be read at such other times which you have of leisure from your domestic employments.

3. Those portions of Scripture which you use in your Prayers, let them not be long. A Chapter at once; no more: but then what time you can afford, spend it in thinking and meditating upon the holy Precepts which you read.

4. Be sure to meditate so long, till you make some act of piety upon the occasion of what you meditate; either that you get some new arguments against a sin, or some new encouragements to virtue; some spiritual strength and advantage, or else some act of Prayer to God, or glorification of him.

5. I advise that you would read your Chapter in the midst of your Prayers in the Morning, if they be divided according to the number of the former actions; because little interruptions will be apt to make your Prayers less tedious, and your self more intent upon them: But if you find any other way

more agreeing to your spirit and disposition, use your liberty without scruple.[8]

We see in Taylor's advice the continuing practice of reading the Bible in the context of some sort of daily private prayer, whether it be one of the monastic offices, the prayer book rites for morning and evening prayer, or some simpler form of daily devotions. As in the church's eucharistic liturgy, the Bible was read as spiritual nourishment, for the purpose of gaining "new encouragements to virtue" or "some spiritual strength and advantage" (as well as the practical purpose of providing "little interruptions" that will make "your Prayers less tedious"), while reading the Bible as a historical or religious text should be done later in the day, when "you have of leisure from your domestic employments."

In his instructions for reading the Bible, Taylor draws on the ancient Jewish practice of *lectio divina* or "sacred reading": moving through the text slowly and meditatively, letting the words sink into the silence and ruminating on them until they are fully "digested." Sacred reading was embraced by the monastics of the early church and became the heart of the Benedictine life of prayer and study. Far from merely seeing or hearing the words on a page, *lectio* is an active form of reading that uses all dimensions of the imagination and intellect to understand the meaning of the text and bring that text alive in one's life in the here and now. It "implies thinking of a thing with the intent to do it; in other words, to prepare oneself for it, to prefigure it in the mind, to desire it, in a way, to do it in advance—briefly, to practice it." This practice of meditation on the words of Scripture "inscribes," as one Benedictine describes it, "the sacred text in the body and in the soul."[9] The focus is not on the quantity of text read—sometimes only a word or phrase is necessary—but rather on entering deeply into the text and discerning its particular meaning for the reader at that point in time. As Jeremy Taylor concludes: "Read not much at a time; but meditate as much as your time, and capacity, and disposition will give you leave: ever remembering, that little reading, and much thinking; little speaking, and much hearing; frequent and short prayers, and great devotion, is the best way to be wise, to be holy, to be devout."[10]

This devotional use of Scripture came under scrutiny with the rise of nineteenth-century German scholarship, which emphasized historical-critical methods of interpreting the Bible. In the Church of England, however, the tension it created between purely devotional reading and critical appreciation of the texts of the Bible was relaxed somewhat through the intellectual leadership of scholarly bishops and teachers of deep devotion, such as Michael Ramsey, C. S. Lewis, William Temple, and Rowan Williams. Nonetheless, the fundamental principles established during the formative years of Anglicanism remain touchstones for Anglicans today. We read the Bible in the context of prayer and the sacraments, whether that be in the lessons read aloud in the Sunday eucharist according to the Revised Common Lectionary or the readings of the prayer book's daily office prayed alone in one's "closet" or with a small group. Anglicans are responsible for interpreting the Bible in community, within the "academy" of the church and in light of the church's tradition, not according to personal whim or pulling verses out of context to make the text say what we wish it to say. In other words, while we affirm the authority and primacy of the Bible as the word of God, we also recognize the interpretive role of the gathered community, one that is performed most effectively in the liturgies and sacraments we share in our common prayer.

"SERMONS ARE DANGEROUS THINGS"

One of the most important ways that Anglicans read and interpret the Bible in community is the sermon. In the early church the Hebrew and Christian scriptures were taught and interpreted through homilies based on the verse-by-verse exposition of a biblical passage. Developed into its classical form in Alexandria by the second-century biblical scholar Origen, the homily was basically a rereading of a particular text from Scripture with a running commentary on each verse or phrase. Often using the method of interpretation known as allegory, which uncovers deeper truths hidden behind the literal meaning of a text, the bishops of the fourth century were trained in schools of rhetoric and brought an eloquence to preaching it had seldom had before; the pastoral sermons of Basil of Caesarea and his brother Gregory of Nyssa, the orations of their friend Gregory of Nazianzus, and the eloquent homilies of Augustine of Hippo are seeing a revival of interest in the church today. Ancient catechetical instruction is also finding new life in the twenty-first-century church as we seek to recover an awareness of the significance of baptism. The baptismal sermons of Ambrose of Milan, Theodore of Mopsuestia, Cyril of Jerusalem, and John Chrysostom (whose eloquence earned him the name "Golden Mouth") all stand the test of time, and despite cultural and theological differences speak a living word today.

With the collapse of the Roman empire and the influx of non-Christian tribes and people, the teaching and preaching needs of the church changed. The Greek and then Latin expository or catechetical sermons of the patristic era were gradually replaced by evangelical sermons preached in the vernacular languages of people who knew little if anything about Christianity. Few of the sermons of English missionaries who traveled to northern Europe, such as Bonifice, who carried the gospel to Germany, and Willibrord, who preached to the Frisians, were written down, but by the time of Charlemagne preaching was an integral part of the effort to socialize the newly Christian Saxons and Franks. The reform councils of 813 insisted that sermons be preached in the language of the people, and those sermons were to set forth a theology that these Christian "newcomers" could understand. Likewise, in England we see in the sermons of the early middle ages an emphasis on preaching as a way of providing basic instruction to new Christians, especially as infant baptism became more common and the teaching previously done during the time of preparation for baptism during Lent was now done through sermons to the entire congregation.

While many people read devotional literature at that time, many more listened to sermons offered in church and on street corners, in monastery cloisters and outdoor theaters. It was an integral part of monastic observance, with sermons offered in chapels and cloisters and at places of outdoor work throughout the day. The observation that the "religious culture of the later middle ages was in large measure a preached culture"[11] can be supported by the sheer number of sermons we have preserved in manuscript form—more than eighty thousand from 1150 to 1350 alone, with many more in outline or note form, and more still simply lost or never written down.[12]

This abundance continued through the Reformation and well into the eighteenth century. Historian O. C. Edwards has commented on the homiletical diet of the Puritans: "It is doubtful that many other groups in history have been so systematically stuffed." With sermons lasting one or two hours in length, twice on Sunday and often once during the week, he calculates that a regular churchgoer in New England would have "listened to something like seven thousand sermons in a lifetime, totaling somewhere around fifteen thousand hours of concentrated listening."[13] An alternative form of the homily—the thematic sermon— added to the variety. In thematic preaching the preacher followed a strict three-part form in which the chosen theme from the Bible was followed by prayer, a repetition of the text, and the development of the theme by the use of stories and illustrations. In times of confusing and conflicting ferment in all things religious, the sermon was both the means and the manifestation of articulating reforming principles and timeless truths. Preaching could also be a source of entertainment; in seventeenth-century England it was more popular than bear-baiting, morris dancing, and Shakespeare.[14] When the famous preacher Phillips Brooks died in 1893, even the Boston stock market closed as thousands of mourners paid their respects at Trinity Church, Copley Square.

Brooks's blend of scholarship, cultural awareness, and deep personal faith contributed to his renown. He warned his fellow preachers to "beware of the tendency to preach about Christianity, and try to preach Christ. To discuss the relations of Christianity and science, Christianity and society, Christianity and politics, is good. To set Christ forth to men so that they shall know him, in gratitude and love become his, that is far better." While it is a good thing to be a messenger who is able to describe the gospel accurately and clearly, he concluded, "it is better to be a Prometheus who brings the sun's fire to the earth."[15]

Like Brooks, contemporary preacher Barbara Brown Taylor sees the sermon as both a *message* to be passed on and a *witness* to the experience of God in the lives of both preacher and hearers. "When the holy vision speaks," Taylor writes, "it is my own heart that is pierced. . . . Every word I choose, every image, every rise in my voice reveals my own involvement in the message." The word that is preached in sermons is thus "embodied" in human lives—in Taylor's memorable phrase, "we are living libraries of God's word." And yet this does not give the preacher permission to talk about herself. Every sermon, good or bad, is always a "variation on someone else's theme. The main melody is always a given, and even when we launch into our own bold improvisations we are limited to a scale of eight notes."[16]

Yet sermons are not always a lively and brilliant word that brings life and compelling insight to bear on the lives of those present. Indeed, many of us can sympathize with the woman in Reformation bishop Hugh Latimer's story who would go to a certain church to listen to the sermons because she needed the sleep. Excellent preaching requires not just an intellectual and experiential grasp of the Christian faith, not just training in biblical interpretation and theology; it also demands a certain facility with the spoken word and a call to personal holiness—to articulating and living out the message one preaches. Eloquence in speaking does not always goes hand in hand with brilliance or skill in crafting a sermon: one observer of the masterful sermons of Richard Hooker remembered that when he preached "his voice was low, stature little, gesture none at all, standing stone-still in the Pulpit." His presentation left much to be desired, for "where his eye was left fixed at the beginning, it was found fixed at the end of his Sermon."[17]

The pressure to offer an interesting performance in preaching is increased today by the fact that we are accustomed to constant stimulation and easy entertainment. Hearing a sermon requires sustained and focused listening skills that are often underdeveloped in those of us who have grown up surfing channels on television and playing high-speed video games, and for whom multitasking with handheld electronic devices is a way of life. In a sermon, observes Taylor, "if the topic is not appealing, there are no other channels to be tried. If a phrase is missed, there is no replay button to be pressed."[18] No wonder many of us find listening to sermons—even good ones—a challenge.

This problem is not new. Sixteen hundred years ago Bishop Augustine of Hippo yearned for students who were eager for knowledge, "however dismally and crudely it is expressed" and who could love "in words what is true, not the words themselves." But when entertainment and eloquence are valued more than substance, Augustine acknowledges, preachers must sometimes spice up their sermons in order to be heard: "Yes, there is a certain similarity between feeding and learning; so because so many people are fussy and fastidious, even those foodstuffs without which life cannot be supported need their pickles and spices."[19]

Earlier ages focused more on the personal holiness of the preacher than we do today, but the call for a renewal in preaching by tending to the spiritual life of the preacher has been heard repeatedly over the course of the church's history. In his book *The Reformed Pastor*, based on the *Worcester Agreement* signed by more than fifty ministers seeking to renew the holiness and spiritual life of the church through preaching, the seventeenth-century parson Richard Baxter urged his fellow clergy to "preach to yourselves the sermons you study before you preach them to others."

> When I let my heart grow cold, my preaching is cold; and when it is confused my preaching is so too: and I can observe the same frequently in the best of my hearers, that, when I have a while grown cold in preaching, they have cooled accordingly; and the next prayers that I have heard from them have been too much like my preaching.

The spiritual life of the preacher does indeed make a difference, Baxter believed, for "if we feed on unwholesome food, either errors or fruitless controversies, our hearers are likely to fare the worse for it. Whereas if we abound in faith, love, and zeal, how will it overflow to the refreshing of our congregations, and how will it appear in the increase of the same graces in others."[20]

Another factor the preacher must take into account when crafting a sermon is the audience. Pope Gregory the Great was one of the first pastors to address the topic of how to preach to a congregation with significant intellectual, economic, and social diversity. His *Pastoral Rule*, written in 591, acknowledges that "one and the same exhortation does not suit all":

> For the things that profit some often hurt others; seeing that also for the most part herbs which nourish some animals are fatal to others; and the gentle hissing that quiets horses incites whelps; and the medicine which abates one disease aggravates another; and the bread which invigorates the life of the strong kills little children.

Preachers ought to fashion their sermons to their congregation, and yet "never deviate from the art of common edification." The way to accomplish this was to seek to "edify all in the one virtue of charity," touching the "hearts of his hearers out of one doctrine," which was expounded with many different exhortations.[21]

In our day, Barbara Brown Taylor adds another important dimension to the art of preaching: the participation of those who listen. She has found that the involvement of the people in the congregation through active listening is an essential aspect of any sermon, and how they respond can make or break a sermon:

> An inspired sermon can wind up skewered somewhere near the second pew by a congregation of people who sit with their arms crossed and their eyes narrowed, coughing and scuffing their feet as the preacher struggles to be heard. Similarly, a weak sermon can grow strong in the presence of people who attend carefully to it, leaning forward in their pews and opening their faces to a preacher from whom they clearly expect to receive good news.[22]

While contemporary preachers are expected to compose an original sermon every week, previous generations accepted the reality that not every person who enters the pulpit is capable of that, and even the best preachers will sometimes find themselves at a loss for meaningful insight. The formidable bishop Augustine of Hippo counseled that when preachers cannot think up anything to say, they should instead read a sermon written by one of the masters. The sermons, treatises, and letters of the early apostles and church fathers were part of the body of written texts that would become the apostolic and biblical tradition to which later generations looked for authentic Christian teaching, and efforts were made throughout the middle ages to preserve and translate these texts for the present day. In England the work of the early eighth-century scholar monk known as the Venerable Bede is of particular note. While Bede is most widely known today for his historical narrative of the English church and people, he considered his work in biblical interpretation of greater significance in furthering the education of the English monks, clergy, and people, and facilitating the evangelization of the Anglo-Saxon church. In addition to almost twenty-five commentaries on the Bible summarizing the patristic interpretations along with his own insights, Bede wrote two books of *Homilies on the Gospels.* These fifty sermons for the Christmas and Easter seasons provide simple outlines in which following a brief introduction the biblical passage is examined not verse by verse but as a whole, followed by a short application of the gospel teaching to the spiritual lives of the listeners.

Some three hundred years later another scholar monk, Aelfric of Eynsham, followed in Bede's footsteps by providing preaching aids for the clergy of his day. A prolific writer, Aelfric collected and translated into Anglo-Saxon the Latin sermons of the church fathers and offered a number of his own compositions. His three series of homilies cover the seasons and feasts of the church year, church doctrine and history, and the lives of the saints. In his translation of the sermons of the church fathers, Aelfric was building upon the collections called "homiliaries" that were popular as the decline of Latin culture meant fewer educated clergy to interpret the scriptures afresh. Rather than attempt to write their own, clerics searched the sermons of the church fathers for insights that could speak to their own generation. These homiliaries, which first appear in Africa at a time when the church was growing too quickly for the bishops to be able to preach everywhere and on every occasion, provided clergy with homilies for the liturgical church year they could read aloud to their congregations, as well as reflective pieces to be read privately for personal study or to serve as a guide when composing their own sermons. The Rule of St. Benedict refers to these homiliaries as auxiliary material for the monks' *lectio divina,* and they seem to have been used especially at the night office. Aelfric used as one of his sources the homiliaries of Paul the Deacon, asked by Charlemagne to edit a collection of homilies as part of his efforts at liturgical and educational reform because the available texts were so corrupt as to be unintelligible. His volume of almost two hundred fifty sermons and homilies for every Sunday and feast day in the liturgical year, including masters of preaching from Bede to Leo the Great, John Chrysostom and Augustine to Gregory the Great, was so remarkable that it was used for a thousand years.

In times of the church's life when the education of the clergy lagged, the use of previously written sermons was considered a helpful way to encourage and improve the quality of learning in the congregation, as well as to teach a particular perspective the clergy were not prepared to offer. In Tudor England, for example, priests were given a *Book of Homilies* that articulated for the congregation the Protestant principles and interpretation of biblical texts of the prevailing church leaders, including Archbishop Cranmer—views many of the clergy were either unable to elucidate or unwilling to espouse. These sermons conveyed the emerging Anglican vision of a Christian commonwealth in which the focus of religion is not so much on a good and holy death as on a human life that improves the human social fabric. Though dissenters objected to the preaching of rote homilies in church, complaining that the "drone of the Homilies replaced the mutter of the Mass," the sermons of *The Book of Homilies* were an essential part of the efforts for widespread education in humanist principles at the heart of the Reformation in England.

The development of preaching aids continued apace with the invention of the printing press, and the Protestant Reformation raised the importance of the sermon to new heights as a means of interpreting salvation in the life of the individual Christian. The evangelical Cambridge teacher of preaching Charles Simeon, for example, taught his students not how to preach the sermons of others, but how to prepare their own by providing a collection of sermon outlines they could follow. His collection grew from one hundred in 1796 to over two thousand outlines on the "preachable texts" of the Bible in the full edition of his *Horae Homileticae*. Many of these classic sermon outlines on biblical texts, illustrations and stories, quotations and "sayings" are incorporated into modern materials on preaching and remain essential elements in the sermon preparation practiced by preachers today, as well as useful resources for personal daily devotion for clergy and laity alike.

Devotional Books

While the words may change over time, books of prayer remain a popular resource for personal devotion among Anglicans today, whether they be monastic offices adapted for personal use or collections of prayers from church tradition. In addition to the daily offices and prayers found in the 1979 Book of Common Prayer and newer Anglican prayer books, volumes of prayers in a wide variety of formats abound, with texts gathered from all generations of Anglican history, from the Celtic and Roman church to the modern day.

Originally copied by hand and richly illustrated, Books of Hours were private devotions that had been adapted from the monastic offices, and included psalms and litanies as well as the "little hours" that developed alongside the communal offices of the day. From the early middle ages on, these prayer books for laity were the beloved heirlooms of the wealthy and were identified in their wills to be passed from one generation to another. By the late fourteenth century, mass-produced volumes from northern France and the Low Countries were available to a wider market of local gentry and merchants; these books were printed on vellum with plain or simply decorated text, along with occasional full-page illustrations purchased by the printer in bulk and "tipped into the volumes to dress them up."[23] By the end of the fifteenth century, with the invention of the printing press richly decorated copies of the Book of Hours could be purchased at a cost afforded even by domestic servants. Multiple copies could be purchased for use by a whole family, as seen in the famous Hans Holbein drawing of the family of Sir Thomas More at prayer.

In the often poignant prayers and abundant notations written in the margins of many of these books, we can see the practice of copying favorite prayers and journaling notes, just as we might make in our own prayer books today. Some Books of Hours had multiple owners over time, with additions made by different hands. In the inexpensive 1530 volume that Thomas More took with him to the Tower during his final imprisonment for refusing to affirm the Act of Supremacy, he wrote a poignant prayer asking for grace "to sett the world at nought" and "to be content to be solitary, not to long for worldely company." More often the annotations are of favorite prayers or notes as to when and where they were prayed with great effect. As the historian Eamon Duffy concludes: "The voice of lay prayer in the late middle ages is essentially ventrilo-quial. By and large, medieval people did not speak for themselves when they prayed. They articulated their hopes and fears, however deeply felt, in the borrowed words of others, which they made their own in the act of recitation."[24]

During the Reformation the Book of Hours, with its prayers to the Virgin Mary and the saints, became a battleground between Catholics and Protestants, and prayers alluding to purgatory, papal authority, or Archbishop Thomas Becket (who had in an earlier century confronted royal authority and won) were often ordered to be removed, blotted, or scratched out during the reigns of Prot-estant rulers. Reformed primers were printed after 1535, such as the Sarum *Horae*, and by 1545 only one Royal Primer was to be used in Henry VIII's realm. Such wholesale changes were long in coming, however, as individuals and families continued to use their beloved texts, and banned volumes were quick to be reversed with changes in the political realm. Nonetheless, although Elizabeth I issued editions of the Book of Hours in 1560, 1565, and 1575, by the end of the sixteenth century the whole notion of saying the "little hours" was increasingly out of step with the English Protes-tant church, though books containing collections of prayers and practices for devotion and the reading of Scripture continued to be printed for personal use.

HISTORIES AND HAGIOGRAPHY

Bibles, prayer books, and devotional treatises were not the only books that nurtured the spiritual lives of Anglicans and their forebears. Just as Scripture was read and interpreted in the context of the liturgy for the purpose of sanctification and growth in holiness, so the lives of exemplary Christians of previous generations were important wit-nesses to the faith. In this sense the narrative of a saint's life is not simply or even primarily intended to be factual or complete, for the purpose of hagiography was to teach and enlighten the hearer, and inspire a new generation to the same holiness of life. Many lives of the saints were written for this reason, to be read during the liturgical offices of the monastery or worship services of the parish church. The lives and teachings of bishops, monks, and missionaries of the early and medieval church—Benedict and Gregory the Great, Boniface and Willibrord, Patrick and Columba, Martin of Tours and Anskar—are remembered in texts that give us a glimpse of the faith as it was lived in their own times and places.

Perhaps the most important source for Anglicans is Bede's *Ecclesiastical History of the English Nation*, which incorporates the sayings and acts of any number of Anglo-Saxon and Celtic Christians into a narrative of the history of the church and culture in which Bede lived. From his monastery in Wearmouth-Jarrow, with its outstanding library of classical texts, Bede set about gathering documents from churches and monasteries—the monks at Canterbury provided letters and texts from Pope Gregory and Archbishop Augustine, for example—and compiling stories and oral histories from individuals who remembered the people and events he was recounting. Bede also included the texts of letters between bishops and kings, missionaries and queens, as well as sermons preached and prayers offered.

Bede wrote his history for the purpose of inspiring people to lives of virtue: "For if history relates good things of good men," he begins, "the attentive hearer is excited to imitate that which is good; or if it mentions evil things of wicked persons, nevertheless the religious and pious hearer or reader, shunning that which is hurtful and perverse, is the more earnestly excited to perform those things which he knows to be good, and worthy of God." Like any historian, Bede then details his sources of information, which included the remembered stories of Abbot Albinus from Canterbury, who knew Archbishop Theodore of Tarsus, one of the successors of Augustine of Canterbury—recalling the ways in which the apostolic tradition of the early church was passed from one generation to another. Other bishops and monks wrote to him of their recollections of the history of their province, and for his own area of Northumbria, Bede collected the "faithful testimony of innumerable witnesses, who remember the same, besides what I had of my own knowledge."[25] Thus we have in Bede's historical account not only the background narrative of many of the pivotal political and social events of that time, but also a record of the life stories, prayers, sermons, and conversations of significant figures of the early English church.

Today we tend to prefer our biographies to be historically accurate and exhaustive in detail, not the exuberant praise of God's power in the lives of the saints and the selective overlooking of their faults by medieval historians. Yet the historian Jean Leclercq reminds us that "every age has its own set of values," and we must take them into account when reading these earlier writers:

> When we admire a Renaissance palace we do not condemn it because living in it may have been uncomfortable. We acknowledge a successful artistic achievement, and we accept the fact that the men of the time may have had a different concept of daily living from ours. In like manner, medieval men took more interest in permanent and universal ideas than in specific events transitory in nature. To understand them, one must adopt their point of view. Once this is done, legend becomes, in a sense they themselves would have approved, truer than history.[26]

The newest edition of this sort of holy biography in the Episcopal Church is *Holy Women, Holy Men*, which includes the vastly increased and widely inclusive list of holy people to be remembered in the church's calendar. It is a response to the church's call for a revision of *Lesser Feasts and Fasts* to affirm "our lively experience of sainthood in local communities."[27] To give just one example, I serve as the deacon of the small parish in Maine at which Frances Perkins worshiped when she was at her home in Newcastle. Perkins's passion for justice for working people led her to become Franklin Delano Roosevelt's secretary of labor and the first woman cabinet member, where she was responsible for crafting many of the social policies that provided needed aid during the Great Depression and beyond, including the Social Security program. Our local "Saint Frances of Newcastle" is now honored on May 13 in the Episcopal calendar, and her lingering presence in the pews and in the work of her grandson, who continues as an active member of the parish, calls us to similar perseverance in the ongoing struggle for social justice in the workplace and financial security for working men and women throughout their lives.

LETTER WRITING AS SPIRITUAL PRACTICE

One of the ways we learn firsthand about the faith and lives of exemplary Christians in their historical context is through the practice of writing letters. A number of the "books" of the New Testament are actually letters that were sent by Paul or one of the other church leaders to a particular community—the church in Corinth or Ephesus, for example. Ignatius, Ireneaus, Polycarp, Clement, and other leaders of the early church similarly wrote letters that were read aloud in worship services and shared among house churches. These epistles addressed the pressing questions of faith that Christians encountered in their daily lives: Do Jewish Christians need to be circumcised and keep the dietary laws of Judaism? Is it acceptable for a Christian to eat the meat that has been sacrificed to an idol? How can a Christian who has offered incense to the emperor in order to avoid persecution be restored to the church community? Local communities saved and revered these letters, and in time they were gathered, along with four of the many gospels that had been written about the life of Jesus, into the canon of texts Christians affirmed as the word of God.

This tradition of letter writing continued throughout the middle ages and beyond; in fact much of what we know about the medieval church is from letters written by missionaries to their bishops for advice on how to handle perplexing cultural differences regarding marriage customs, or by bishops seeking clarification on what to do about clergy who baptized according to different formulas than Rome. The monasteries too produced an abundant supply of letters between monks and nuns, and from those seeking advice or spiritual direction. As Dom Jean Leclercq has noted, letter writing was a literary form prized by the monastics because "this way of conversing through the written word harmonized with the silence enjoined by the *Rule*, with the vow of stability, and with cloistered life."[28] The monasteries even developed a postal service among themselves, with countless carriers moving among the abbeys of medieval Europe bringing announcements written on long parchment strips to which new pieces would be sewn, as well as letters of support, counsel, or condolence.

While such letters communicated all sorts of information and served many different purposes throughout the middle ages and beyond, they were also an important means of spiritual guidance and friendship. One more recent example of this practice are the letters of Evelyn Underhill, a twentieth-century English scholar and retreat leader who carried on a vibrant ministry of spiritual direction through the written word. In her letters she would recommend particular books to read from the classics and her own day, as well as advice on spiritual practices to embrace or try, all in a spirit of practical, loving care and down-to-earth common sense. She urged those who tended to take their religious experience to the point of exclusive obsession to "remember you have no more right to be extravagant over this than over any other pleasure or craving."[29] When she thought the focus was rather too much on sin and not enough on grace, she counseled:

> I feel like writing you a rather bracing, disagreeable, east-windy sort of letter. When I read yours my first impulse was to send you a line begging you only to *let yourself alone*. Don't keep on pulling yourself to pieces: and please burn that dreadful book with the list of your past sins! If the past really oppresses you, you had far better go to confession, and finish that chapter once and for all! It is emphatically your business now to look forwards and not backwards: and also to look forwards in an eager and optimistic spirit. Any other course is mere ingratitude, you know.[30]

Underhill drew upon her own experience of prayer and devotion, which was deeply sacramental and mystical while also rooted in the church's traditions and practices. When one inquirer wrote in despair while in the depths of an experience of the absence of God, Underhill well understood the anguish of such a "dark night of the soul," but offered this reassuring advice about a "normal experience in spiritual growth":

Don't struggle with prayer you can't do—just say "Into thy hands I commend my spirit." Continue your Communions quite steadily but don't pull yourself to bits over them. Remember it is you who are temporarily blinded, not the world that has gone black. Early bed, novels, the flicks and so on are all good and help to minimize the nervous strain. Do not be too ferocious in your exercises in detachment at the moment, and try not to be discouraged, though I know this is hard. Your grief at God's absence is the best of all proofs of your love.[31]

In a similar vein, she urged paying attention to nurturing a wholeness and breadth in the spiritual life that encompasses all parts of human life and culture, not just the religious dimensions. "Consider the sequence of daily acts, and your external interests as part of your service, part of God's order for you," she advised another inquirer, "and as having a proper claim on your undivided attention." Underhill urged him to develop his interest in music, and to work at it as a necessary obligation for his spiritual health: "You will very soon find," she reassured him, "that it has a steadying effect." While she spurred some on to undertake a more serious practice of the spiritual life, she counseled balance and rest for this intensely religious young Christian:

> Just for the present, do go as quietly as you can, about your work, etc., I mean. Avoid strain. If you could take a few days off and keep quite quiet it would be good, but if this is impossible at any rate go along gently, look after your body, don't saturate yourself the whole time with mystical books. I know you do feel tremendously stimulated all round; but remember the "young presumptuous disciple" in the *Cloud*! Hot milk and a thoroughly foolish novel are better things for you to go to bed on just now than St. Teresa.[32]

Throughout Underhill's letters we see the Anglican emphasis on spirituality and prayer practiced in a balanced and ordered life within the context of Christian community. "*Anyone* can 'lead a prayer-life,'" she told one inquirer. "This only involves making a suitable rule and making up your mind to keep it however boring this may be." Yet this rule is not kept in isolation, but in the midst of and supported by the church, the body of Christ. "If dryness and distractions have you in their clutches just now, fall back on the Divine Office," she urged, "with the *intention* of joining the great corporate prayer of the Church." Remember that "you are only a unit in the Chorus of the Church and not responsible for a solo part," Underhill concluded, "so that the others will make good the shortcomings you cannot help."[33]

Underhill's phrase "the Chorus of the Church" draws on a very Anglican sense of the communion of the saints in every time and place, in which the gifts of each member of the body of Christ are freely given in love for the good of the whole world. And so it is to the church as the community of disciples called to love one another that we turn in the next chapter.

ANGLICAN VOICES ON PROCLAIMING THE WORD

The gifts and books you have sent us have been received with a joyful and grateful heart. With hands upraised to heaven we beseech the Supreme Majesty to repay you with an ample reward amongst the angels in heaven. But now we beg Your Holiness with earnest prayer that in your kindness and affection you would deign to pray for us in our struggles and trials. The great burden that weighs upon us compels us to seek the help of good men, as it is written: "The earnest prayer of the just man availeth much." The brevity of this letter, however, prevents us from telling you all the ills we suffer both within and without.

For the present, we beg you from the bottom of our hearts to comfort us in our sorrow, as you have done before, by sending us a spark from that light of the Church which the Holy Spirit has kindled in your land; in other words, be so kind as to send us some of the works which Bede, the inspired priest and student of Sacred Scripture, has composed—in particular, if it can be done, his book of homilies for the year (because it would be a very handy and useful manual for us in our preaching), and the Proverbs of Solomon. We hear that he has written commentaries on this book. . . .

Finally, we are sending you by the bearer of this letter two small casks of wine, asking you in token of our mutual affection to use it for a merry day with the brethren. We beg you so to treat our requests that your reward may shine forth in the heavens.

—A letter from Boniface to Archbishop Egbert asking for
the works of Bede (ca 747–751)

He cannot take to the plow? Then let him take up the pen; it is much more useful. In the furrows he traces on the parchment, he will sow the seeds of the divine words. . . . He will preach without opening his mouth; without breaking silence, he will make the Lord's teaching resound in the ears of the nations; and without leaving his cloister, he will journey far over land and sea.

—Peter the Venerable, writing of scholar-monks,
Epistle I.20 (12th century)

In a word, the Apostles Preaching was therefore mighty, and successful, because plain, natural, and familiar, and by no means above the Capacity of their Hearers: nothing being more preposterous than for those, who were professedly aiming at Men's *Hearts*, to miss the Mark, by shooting *over their Heads*.

—Robert South, "Christ's Promises to
the Apostles" (1676)

O Lord, we come this morning
Knee-bowed and body-bent
Before thy throne of grace.
O Lord—this morning—
Bow our hearts beneath our knees,
And our knees in some lonesome valley,
We come this morning—
Like empty pitchers to a full fountain,
With no merits of our own,
O Lord—open up a window of heaven,

And lean out far over the battlements of glory,
And listen this morning.

> —James Weldon Johnson, "Listen, Lord—A Prayer" from
> *God's Trombones* (1927)

Being fully human in the pulpit does not mean telling personal stories or making oneself the focus, but something much deeper and more difficult. It is about bringing all of oneself—body, mind, and spirit—to the preaching task, to the encounter with God that takes place in preaching. Rather than seeking to "get out of the way" of God's Word, to become an empty channel or a transparent window, I experience my task as a preacher to be the challenge of coming as fully as possible into myself, into my body, my voice, and my presence in the room with a group of listeners. . . . Then God takes my words and makes of them something much holier than I can do by myself.

> —Ruthanna B. Hooke, *Transforming Preaching* (2010)[34]

QUESTIONS FOR REFLECTION AND DISCUSSION

1. What does the Bible mean to you now? Has that changed over time? How do you learn the words of Scripture best? In what ways does your knowledge of the Bible encourage you to "proclaim by word and example the Good News of God in Christ"?

2. Describe a memorable experience in which you heard a sermon that changed your life in some way. What was it that made such an impression on you: the preacher's delivery? the particular words the preacher used? the situation in which the sermon was given? How did your own "active listening" and the involvement of others who were listening to the sermon affect what you heard?

3. What other forms of spiritual practice involving the written or spoken word have made a difference in your life? How do they inform your ability to proclaim the gospel in your daily life?

Seeking Christ in Community

Will you seek and serve Christ in all persons, loving your neighbor as yourself? (BCP 305)

"Most of our brother Christians showed unbounded love and loyalty, never sparing themselves and thinking only of one another," Bishop Dionysius of Alexandria wrote in the midst of a ravaging epidemic of smallpox in the mid-third century. In contrast to the "heathen" who left the cities and "fled from their dearest, throwing them into the roads before they were dead," leaving the dead unburied and the sick to fend for themselves, Dionysius praised the many Christians who remained behind and "took charge of the sick, attending to their every need and ministering to them in Christ, and with them departed this life serenely happy; for they were infected by others with the disease, drawing on themselves the sickness of their neighbors and cheerfully accepting their pains." Indeed, the bishop believed these Christians, "in nursing and curing others, transferred their death to themselves and died in their stead." Thus even though the church lost a large number of presbyters, deacons, and lay people to the plague, through their willingness to remain with the sick and dying and care for them to the end, Dionysius concluded, the death of these Christians, "the result of great piety and strong faith, seems in every way the equal of martyrdom."[1]

Sixteen hundred years later, their story would be echoed halfway around the world in 1878 in Memphis, Tennessee, as terrified residents fled the yellow fever epidemic in the city on foot, in carriages, wagons, carts, and trains. "The scene I witnessed at the depot could not be pictured," recalled one resident fleeing to Louisville. "We were nearly crushed in obtaining our places. At last the over-crowded train moved off amid the loud and heartrending cries of those left behind. I was told that a child and an old person were trampled to death near us on the platform." Everyone who had the means to leave did so, leaving the sick, the poor, and the infirm to fend for themselves. Only a very few were travelling in the opposite direction and choosing to enter the infected city. Two of these travelers were Sister Constance and Sister Thecla. When they heard of the outbreak while resting during the summer school vacation at their Episcopal convent in Peekskill, New York, they lost no time in securing supplies and returning to St. Mary's School in Memphis. When they arrived and were told for their own safety they would be sleeping in the country, out of the infected atmosphere, and working in the town only during the day, they rejected the idea outright, saying, "We cannot listen to such a plan; it would never do; we are going to nurse day and night; we must be at our post."

The tasks associated with nursing so many critically ill people were overwhelming, especially for teachers who were not trained as nurses or physicians. On August 29, 1878, Constance described her day in a letter to her Mother Superior:

> Yesterday I found two young girls, who had spent two days in a two-room cottage with the unburied bodies of their parents, their uncle in the utmost suffering and delirium, and no one near them but a rough negro drayman who held the sick man in his bed. It was twenty-four hours before I could get those two fearful corpses buried, and then I had to send for a police officer to the Board of Health, before any undertaker would enter that room. One grows perfectly hardened to these things— carts, with eight or nine corpses in rough boxes, are ordinary sights. I saw a nurse stop one to-day and ask for a certain man's residence—the negro driver just pointed over his shoulder with his whip at the heap of coffins behind him and answered, "I've got him here in his coffin."

In the midst of such overwhelming suffering, Constance and Thecla, along with several other Sisters of St. Mary and Episcopal clergy of the local parishes, cared unceasingly for the sick and dying, the orphans and elderly, until they too succumbed to the virulent disease. Louis Sanford Schuyler, an Episcopal priest who left his church in New Jersey to assist in the efforts, arrived on September 8, just as Constance and Thecla were themselves stricken by yellow fever; he too would die in the coming days. This small band of Episcopalians led by Sister Constance became known as the Martyrs of Memphis, and are remembered every year in the Episcopal church calendar on September 9, the date of Constance's death.

Why would these Christians willingly place themselves in harm's way, in order to care for people whom they did not even know? In a letter written to the priest's father by members of Louis Schuyler's parish in New Jersey, those who knew him wrote of his care for the people of Memphis during those dark days: "His beautiful and gracious life was a humble imitation of Jesus Christ. He taught us by example the Divine precept, 'Love is the fulfilling of the law.' Now he has perfectly wrought out the Divine ideal and authoritative definition of love—'Greater love hath no man than this, that a man lay down his life for his friends.'"[2] The clergy and sisters of Memphis, like the Christians who stayed behind to care for smallpox victims in Alexandria sixteen centuries before, were fulfilling the law of love preached by Jesus, laying down their lives for others.

In these unusually stark examples, we see the essence of what made Christians distinctive and different from their neighbors. While benevolence and good works are practiced by people of any number of religious faiths or with no religious faith at all, because of our belief in the incarnate life of God in Jesus our care for others is part of our worship and spirituality: in loving other people we are loving Christ himself. This mandate is expressed in the ancient Levitical commandment to "love your neighbor as yourself," which Jesus affirmed to be at the very heart of the gospel, alongside the commandment to love the Lord with all our heart and soul and mind and strength. It can be clearly heard in the story

Jesus told his disciples about the last judgment, when the righteous who appear before the throne are blessed for giving the king food when he was hungry, drink when he was thirsty, welcome when he was a stranger, clothing when he was naked, care when he was sick, and companionship when he was a prisoner. When in their confusion they ask when they have done such things for him, the king replies, "Truly I tell you, just as you did it to one of the least of these who are members of my family, you did it to me" (Matt. 25:31–46).

It is this mandate to care for "the least of these" that lies behind the fourth question asked in the Baptismal Covenant: *Will you seek and serve Christ in all persons, loving your neighbor as yourself?* The ways Anglicans have lived out this vow to love Christ in all people are infinitely varied and specific to every time and place, but the fundamental principle undergirding the question is the Christian imperative to live as community with one another. "For just as the body is one and has many members," Paul wrote to the Christians in Corinth, "and all members of the body, though many, are one body, so it is with Christ. For in the one Spirit we were all baptized into one body—Jews or Greeks, slaves or free—and we were all made to drink of one Spirit" (1 Cor. 12:12–13). We are the body of Christ in the world, and just as we are called to worship God in community, we are called to love one another as God in Christ has loved us. "If one member suffers, all suffer together with it," Paul concluded. "If one member is honored, all rejoice together with it" (1 Cor. 12:26). We do not practice our faith in isolation because we are all parts—members—of the same body.

It is popular today to claim to be "spiritual but not religious," which usually means a purely private relationship with God, one that does not involve sharing one's spiritual life with other people or worshiping in a religious community. Within this belief system it is possible to speak of the mountains or the golf course as one's "chapel," since God is also encountered in the beauty of nature or companionship with friends. Such a separation of an individual believer from the body of the church, however, would have been difficult for Christians in earlier generations to understand. From its very beginnings the church has been a communal institution, and has seen this call to live in loving community mirrored in its experience of God as a Trinity of three persons known in the tradition as Father, Son, and Holy Spirit.

Whether gathering in a home where "two or three" give thanks to God for daily food and safe haven, in a monastic cloister filled with holy silence and prayer in the sharing of a common life, in a rural parish church alive with the voices of children and the wisdom of the elderly, or in a magnificent cathedral resounding with the praise of choirs, Christians have found comfort, strength, and challenge in the company of others who have embarked on the journey of faith. It is in just such communities that the spiritual disciplines of prayer and confession have been practiced, repentance and renewal experienced, sacraments received, and belief in the God of Jesus Christ taught, learned, and affirmed. In this chapter we will look at some of the ways Anglicans have provided for a rich and varied community life in various times and places, and the spiritual practices that make life in community possible and fruitful.

THE PRACTICE OF HOSPITALITY

At the heart and soul of all the various forms Christian community has taken over the centuries is the call to practice the hospitality of God. This is the hospitality of the father who runs to embrace the prodigal son and welcomes him home with a feast (Luke 15:20–24). It is the hospitality of the God who continually reminds his people to "love the stranger" and provide them with food and clothing, "for you were strangers in the land of Egypt" (Deut. 10:18–19). Jesus himself practiced a radical hospitality that crossed the established social boundaries of class, economic status, and gender when he shared meals with the poor and outcast, when he encouraged women and people who were not acceptable to the religious establishment of his day to become his disciples. And he called his disciples to do likewise when he gave them a new commandment to love one another in the same way that he has loved them. Indeed, love was to be the identifying mark of a follower of Jesus: "By this everyone will know that you are my disciples," he told them, "if you have love for one another" (John 13:34–35).

And in some times and in some places the church has been able to live in communities that provide such welcome, compassion, and care. Apparently the Christian practice of hospitality was one of the primary motivators for conversion in the early church, offering a compelling vision of a God who welcomed all into a kingdom of peace and justice, love and mercy. It was also this effort to create a new sort of community based on principles of loving care for the poor and frail, the friendless and the needy, that elicited the scorn of others and the threat of persecution by the Roman authorities. "It is our care of the helpless, our practice of loving kindness that brands us in the eyes of our many opponents," wrote the African theologian Tertullian. "'Only look,' they say, 'look how they love one another!'"[3]

The vision of a community in which all were embraced in love and mercy and the needs of any were met by the abundance of all quickly became obscured by the all-too-familiar barriers of dissension and division, fear and greed. The letters of the apostle Paul attest to the difficulties encountered by any group of Christians attempting to live out the call to love our neighbor as Christ loves us. Anyone who has even visited a Christian congregation today is well aware of the church's inability to live out to the full the vision of the kingdom of God. And yet hospitality is in one sense the primary spiritual practice required of every Christian community. "Hospitality is the practice that keeps the church from becoming a club, a members-only society," writes Diana Butler Bass in her recent *People's History of Christianity*.[4] It is the radical welcome of Jesus, in his concern for the poor and orphaned, the lost sheep and the prodigal sons—"the least of these who are members of my family"—that remains the clarion call to the church to embody the hospitality of God, and the spiritual discipline that must guide all aspects of its common life.

In his sixth-century rule of life for his monastic community at Monte Cassino that would become extraordinarily influential in the western church of the middle ages and into our own day, Benedict of Nursia speaks often of the quality of hospitality that was to be practiced in Benedictine houses. "All who arrive as guests are to be welcomed like Christ," he mandates in chapter 53, "for he is going to say, 'I was a stranger and you welcomed me.'" Benedict goes on to describe what this hospitable welcome entailed, including praying with guests upon their arrival and addressing them with "the greatest humility" and honor: "Let Christ who is received in them be adored with bowed head or prostrate body." Guests were given a companion to guide them through the community's daily prayer, and their bodily needs tended to after their long journey. Their hands and feet were washed by the abbot on behalf of the community, and the abbot was even given leave to break his normal fast so that the hungry traveler would not have to eat alone. This respect and care was to be offered in particular to the poor and those on pilgrimage, "for in them especially is Christ received; for the awe felt for the wealthy imposes respect enough of itself."

Benedict is thus practical and direct in his call to welcome the stranger who arrives at the gates of the monastery, aware that special care must be taken to see Christ in those the world does not esteem as highly. "Here is a glimpse of the reality of love in action," Esther de Waal writes in her now-classic commentary on the Rule of Benedict for our lives today:

> It is only too easy to keep the lines "Let everyone that comes be received as Christ" pinned up above the sink in the kitchen as some sort of pleasing pious ideal; it is very much more difficult, whenever the doorbell rings or the telephone goes or people arrive unexpectedly for a meal, for me actually to *be* there, and to put that into practice by greeting them with my whole self. . . . Hospitality means more than simply the open door, and the place at table; it means warmth, acceptance, enjoyment in welcoming whoever has arrived.[5]

And yet Benedict also places boundaries on the practice of hospitality: the abbot has a separate kitchen for the purpose of entertaining guests so that others might not be disturbed. In this way the common life of the monks is kept intact, preserved from the inevitable disruption, noise, unsettledness, and confusion the arrival of guests must bring. That is why one contemporary rule affirms the need for limits to the hospitality offered by a monastic community, noting, "The claims of our life together and our other ministries mean we cannot take in everyone who wants to come or meet a guest's every need. If we let our life as a brotherhood be overwhelmed by the claims of guests we could endanger the resources by which we can serve them."[6]

Esther de Waal echoes this need for the observance of boundaries that protect the peace and silence of the monastery when she writes, "St. Benedict is careful to impose limits so that the life and work of the monastery can go on—and that of course will ensure that the guest experiences the place as it truly is. Too great a merging of monks and guest will benefit neither. The liturgy after all is pointing to the same principle. Time and space must always be kept so that the monk can encounter God."[7] Those of us who live in towns with large numbers of "summer residents" and vacationing families know this challenge well. It is imperative to preserve the quality of peace and gentle pace of life sought by our visitors, so that the very way of life these guests seek is not destroyed by their numbers and the natural disturbances of travel and noise.

Parish churches likewise encounter challenges to maintain the boundaries of a healthy community life in their practice of hospitality, whether it is in the welcome extended to guests who join in Sunday worship or to those who arrive during the week seeking financial assistance, food and a hot shower, pastoral counseling, or help in locating a safe place to live. Newcomers may need to be helped through the maze of liturgical books in Episcopal worship, or to be assured they are welcome to receive communion; outreach ministries in the community may need to be strengthened or adapted to new circumstances. At a deeper level, hospitality in the parish may involve offering services of worship in a different language or removing barriers such as stairs or narrow doors. It may mean honoring and recognizing the capacity for leadership of members who have been overlooked or silenced in the past, or including as equal members those who might have been avoided because of economic, racial, or social differences. At the same time, the offering of hospitality without some measure of restraint and care can drain a community of its resources and exhaust the members to the point they no longer have a vibrant common life into which they can welcome others. Benedict's call to receive Christ in the guest and stranger is not always easy or clear, but for centuries parishes and monastic communities alike have found their faith deepened and their life renewed by the practice of hospitality, because it centers us once again in the essence of the gospel, close to the heart of the God who welcomes all in love.

THE PRACTICE OF STABILITY

Although many Episcopalians today are not even aware of the presence of Anglican monastic orders, of all the forms of community life practiced in the Christian tradition it could be argued that the Benedictine has been the most formative for Anglicans, both through its monastic establishments and in its influence on our congregational structures and patterns. When Pope Gregory the Great began his reform of the sixth-century church, he incorporated Benedictine principles into church life at all levels, introducing choirs to lead the singing of the liturgy, emphasizing preaching, and holding up the monastic way of life as accessible for all who wished to follow in their path of care and service to others and regular prayer.

According to historian Diana Butler Bass, "the ultimate model of medieval spirituality became the parish church infused with the devotion of the monastery." Gregory and Benedict lived at a time when the world as they knew it had collapsed, and new structures were urgently needed to sustain Christian faith and the stability of the church. Gregory took Benedict's way of life in community and applied it to local communities of worship. "Instead of abandoning religious communities in favor of some sort of personal spiritual quest," Bass asserts, Gregory and Benedict "attended to the need for and the patterning of Christian congregations. Arguably, Christianity would not have survived the fall of Rome without their innovative restructuring of church."[8] It was this sort of restructuring of the local church that was brought to England by Gregory's missionary monk, Augustine of Canterbury.

In Anglo-Saxon England larger churches called "cathedrals" served as the bases from which missionary priests would go out to preach Christianity to the non-Christian inhabitants of a region. These mother-churches were led by groups of clergy, including vicars and multiple curates and chaplains. They existed alongside the monastic communities and the smaller "minsters" and private chapels established by local leaders such as the Saxon nobles, by Christian bishops, or by a group of lay Christians. The seventh-century bishop Wilfrid, for example, led a large Northumbrian diocese of churches that also included the minsters of York, Hexham, and Ripon, where he served as abbot. These and other "minster-places" were a sort of "monastic federation" that did not always follow diocesan lines, and remain an enduring legacy from early Christian England.

The church's expansion during the centuries between Augustine and the Norman Conquest was seriously and repeatedly hampered by the upheavals in society brought about by the Scandinavian incursions and other conquests of neighboring peoples. But by the eleventh century, the building of new parish churches was possible to the extent that Bishop Hereman of Ramsbury could tell the pope in 1050 that England was "being filled everywhere with churches which daily were being added anew in new places."[9] The shift from a network of minsters and mother-churches to local parishes within a diocese was greatly strengthened by twelfth-century bishops who built a framework of rural parishes led by country parsons, beginning in the eastern and southern parts of England and then moving westward and northward, that would remain the iconic image of Anglican churches even into our own day. In fact, most of the local parish churches in England at the Industrial Revolution existed as early as 1180.[10]

For this reason the organizational structure of "one priest, one parish" would be most influential throughout the formative years of the English Reformation and be brought to the New World in the churches of the American colonists. Historically in many parts of the English church these parishes were considered geographical units—that is, people were members of the geographical parish or neighborhood in which they lived, and attended the church located there. Since in earlier times people tended not to be as mobile as we are today, this practice of worshiping alongside one's neighbors for years if not an entire lifetime led to a stability of community life that is not easily found now, when people are accustomed to having a choice in which church to attend, whether it is in their neighborhood or not.

The freedom we enjoy today to choose the community in which we will worship and practice our faith has certain advantages. We can align ourselves with people who share our understanding of God or our interests in social justice or who speak our language or provide the social services we need. On the other hand, that freedom has also given rise to a "church shopping" mentality in which members move from congregation to congregation in search of the most charismatic rector or the most interesting sermons or the most active church school. Rather than putting down church roots in the local neighborhood where we live and work, therefore, we keep our faith "travel-ready" just like our laptops and cell phones, so when the urge to move on strikes us we can pull up stakes easily and go to the next parish.

Such variations in the ways we have perceived the role of a stable community in the life of faith are far from new. In his sixth-century rule of life establishing "a school of the Lord's service," Benedict identifies four different kinds of monks: brothers who live in one monastery under the authority of a rule and abbot for life; solitaries who leave the world to live alone in the desert; monastics who live in small groups without an abbot or rule to guide them; and mendicants who travel from town to town and monastery to monastery, seeking hospitality from others. It is for the first group that Benedict writes his rule, as he seeks to design an orderly environment and pattern of community life in which each person can learn to live his or her commitment to God in daily life to the full. And it is perhaps this first group that has the most to teach those of us living in parishes today about the spiritual practice of stability in the Christian life.

In his comparatively balanced and gentle rule, Benedict hoped to "establish nothing that is harsh or oppressive," while understanding that the monastic way of life could be felt to be "narrow at the beginning" and difficult to sustain over time. Stability and perseverance are necessary virtues for monks following his rule to practice, "for as we progress in this our way of life and in faith, our hearts shall expand, and we shall run the way of God's commandments with the unspeakable sweetness of love."[11] Benedict thus turned away from the extreme physical austerity of many of the rules of other monastic and desert communities of his day, as well as from the idea of the monastic life as a private search for perfection in which seekers move from one monastery to the next hoping to find the ideal life they are looking for. "The Rule does not call us to heroic deeds," writes Esther de Waal in her second commentary on Benedict's Rule, *Living with Contradiction*. "Instead St. Benedict is telling me that my way to God lies in the daily and the ordinary. If I cannot find God here and now, in my home and in my work, in my daily routine, in the things that I handle in the kitchen or in the office, then it is no good looking for him anywhere else."[12] Others have described the Benedictine life as "ordinary life, lived extraordinarily well." The monks followed an ordered daily life of prayer and reading, work and rest. They were to care for all things well as holy gifts, whether they be the tools of the workshop, the vessels on the altar, or their own bodies.

Benedict's monks lived in one community for life unless there was good reason for moving to another monastery or leaving the monastic life entirely, and it was this stability that allowed them to practice the spiritual disciplines that made maturity in the Christian faith possible. In his address to the "Shaping Holy Lives" 2003 conference on Benedictine spirituality, Archbishop Rowan Williams explores this aspect of fidelity within community life as a necessary condition for spiritual maturity. "The promise to live in stability is the most drastic way imaginable of recognizing the otherness of others—just as in marriage," he said. "If the other person is there, ultimately, on sufferance or on condition, if there is a time-expiry dimension to our relations with particular others, we put a limit on the amount of otherness we can manage." But when we remove the possibility of abandoning relationships if the road becomes too difficult, then we are able to do the hard work of growing in holiness within the community of faith, which

Archbishop Williams describes as "an unselfconscious getting used to others." He writes:

> At the very start, then, of thinking about Benedictine holiness, there stands a principle well worth applying to other settings, other relationships—not least the Church itself. How often do we think about the holiness of the Church as bound up with a habitual acceptance of the otherness of others who have made the same commitment? And what does it feel like to imagine holiness as an unselfconscious getting used to others? The presence of the other as a tool worn smooth and grey in the hand? The prosaic settledness of some marriages, the ease of an old priest celebrating the eucharist, the musician's relation to a familiar instrument playing a familiar piece—these belong to the same family of experience as the kind of sanctity that Benedict evokes here.

Such relationships are quiet and undemonstrative, Williams says, "because there is nothing to prove." Benedict does not hold up stability as a goal, furthermore, but the means to that end: "an environment where the long-term sameness of my company will not breed bitterness, cynicism and fear of openness with one another."[13] It is well worth pondering how the practice of stability might enable the deepening of spiritual growth in our own lives and particular communities today.

MONASTIC COMMUNITIES IN ENGLAND

Benedictine monastic traditions were brought to England by Augustine of Canterbury in 597, who established the monastery of Saint Peter and Saint Paul (later named St. Augustine's) in Canterbury along the Benedictine patterns of his own monastery in Rome, St. Andrew's. Within a short time a different pattern of monastic community was also established in Northumbria, as Aidan, Cuthbert, and other Celtic missionary monks from Iona established communities on the "holy island" of Lindisfarne, and Benedict Biscop laid the foundations for monasteries in Jarrow and Wearmouth, where the historian Bede would be brought as a child. A number of monastic houses were built throughout the British Isles in the seventh century, based on both the Benedictine rule and on other monastic rules from houses in western Gaul and Ireland. It was an age of evangelizing bishops and missionaries, all of whom were monks; in the words of historian David Knowles, "the conversion of England and the establishment of the church had been due at every stage to monks."[14]

The Scandinavian invasions effectively put an end to monastic life in Anglo-Saxon England by the end of the ninth century, as one by one the monasteries were sacked, their goods plundered, their monks scattered or killed. It would not return until the revival of monastic life under Archbishop Dunstan of Canterbury a century later. Yet even in their ruined state these earlier monastic communities continued to influence the English church and played an important role in its revival. The ancient sites remained holy in the memories of the church, and the writings of the Venerable Bede kept alive the traditions and stories of Aidan and Cuthbert, Paulinus and Wilfrid, Hilda and Columba, Theodore and Hadrian, for generations to come. Even a cursory glance at the many books on Celtic spirituality available to us today shows the continuing influence these early monastic traditions have on the prayer, worship, and spiritual life in our own church communities. Bede's tribute to the Abbess Hilda could also be said of many of these medieval saints, whose "wonderful devotion and grace" and "example of holy life" was known to the members of her community, but who "also brought about the amendment and salvation of many living at a distance, who heard the inspiring story of her industry and goodness."[15]

Hilda is most famous for her leadership at the Synod of Whitby in 664, called to discuss the different Roman and Celtic methods for the dating of Easter. She was the perfect host for the occasion, for she blended the mingling of traditions in her own life. Born an Anglo-Saxon princess, converted to the Christian faith by Paulinus, the first bishop of the Northumbrians, and raised in churches in Kent and East Anglia that followed the Roman traditions, at age thirty-three Hilda was given a tract of land on the River Wear by the Irish bishop Aidan, "where she observed the monastic rule with a handful of companions." She was soon made abbess of the monastery of Heruteu (Hartlepool), and with Aidan's guidance established a regular observance there, and later founded another monastery at Strenaeshalch (Whitby). Bede describes her work there with admiration:

> She established the same regular life as in her former monastery, and taught the observance of righteousness, mercy, purity, and other virtues, but especially of peace and charity. After the example of the primitive Church, no one there was rich, no one was needy, for everything was held in common, and nothing was considered to be anyone's personal property. So great was her prudence that not only ordinary folk, but kings and princes used to come and ask her advice in their difficulties and take it.[16]

Hilda also provided teaching in the study of Scripture and prepared a number of students for holy orders, five of whom later became bishops. In Hilda's life and work we see the hallmarks of monastic life of that time, with its close connection to the political leaders of the day. We also see the important role these monastic Christians played in local communities, and their emphasis on learning, prayer, and wisdom, as well as economic development and a concern for the material needs of all.

Following the tenth-century revival of monastic life under the leadership of Dunstan of Canterbury, Benedict's "way of life" became the predominant rule for monastic communities throughout the west until the middle of the twelfth century, when the houses of other monastic orders such as the Cistercians and Franciscans, Augustinians and Premonstratensians, Cluniacs and Dominicans began to flourish as well. The growth of monastic communities in England once more came to a shuddering halt at the time of Henry VIII, who made himself the supreme head of the English church—including the monasteries—at the time of his marriage to Anne Boleyn. His dissolution of the monasteries and absorption of their wealth, along with the destruction or sale of their property, enriched the crown but effectively put an end to monastic communities within the emerging Anglican Church for three hundred years. Monks and nuns were given pensions and expected to live apart from their community; some continued to adhere to their vows quietly and unnoticed in local towns and villages, but a significant number were imprisoned, tortured, and killed for their refusal to accept the terms of these "reforms." Monastery buildings and churches were either destroyed, sold, or given to friends of the crown, or converted to other uses.

Opportunities to live an ordered community life were not entirely absent during the three hundred years in which monasticism was lost to the Anglican Church. One such effort was found at Little Gidding, which in the seventeenth century flourished as a lay community of men, women, and children under the leadership of Nicholas Ferrar (a friend of the poet and priest George Herbert) and his mother Mary Ferrar. In the midst of the plague of 1625, the Ferrar extended family bought and refurbished the manor of Little Gidding, restoring its chapel and buildings and seeking to live a rule of life that included the praying of daily offices, the reading of Scripture, the teaching of children, the binding of books, and other manual labors. Meals were accompanied by readings from books of English history or travel. "Mr. Ferrar introduced another piece of ancient Christian discipline," the author of one memoir notes, a service of "vigils" during which one or two members of the community would keep watch in prayer and read the Psalms. An earlier biographer commented that this was "an exercise almost lost in this drowsy age of ours,"[17] an observation that no doubt would be true of many of the other ancient and monastic practices at the time. "If the dense clouds of popery had been dispersed," this biographer complained, "the fogs of an incipient laxity in church discipline and morality had also collected."[18] It was this perceived laxity in the common and devotional life of the local churches that encouraged the formation of distinctive communities like Little Gidding. Still more alternative forms of semimonastic life were the informal houses of lay brethren, modeled after the thirteenth and fourteenth century Beguines of the Low Countries, and the small house churches of the Methodist movement. These groups lived in community but without formal vows.

The Anglo-Catholic revival of the nineteenth century prompted the renewal of monastic life in England and other parts of the Anglican Communion, including the United States, beginning with communities of sisters who provided care for the sick and elderly, orphans and the poor. Sister Constance and Sister Thecla, who gave their lives for the people of Memphis, were members of the Community of St. Mary in New York, founded in 1865 as the first Anglican sisterhood in the Episcopal Church. A number of Episcopal orders of men and women were founded in subsequent decades, some with ties to houses in England, such as the Society of St. John the Evangelist in Cambridge, Massachusetts, whose English branch was established by R. W. Benson in the town of Cowley near Oxford in 1866. Others are new establishments, such as the Order of St. Helena for women and the Order of Julian of Norwich, a mixed order of men and women. These monastic orders often sustain many oblates and associates, retreatants, and those under spiritual direction, who far surpass the number of professed brothers and sisters and carry the influence of the monastic communities into their own parish churches throughout the Anglican Communion.

THE PRACTICE OF RECONCILIATION

"Each day brings fresh opportunities to fulfill the commandment of Christ 'that you love one another as I have loved you,'" the new rule of the Society of St. John the Evangelist affirms. Yet "breaches of trust, injuries, even enmity are bound to happen," tempting us to "defer reconciliation, or even to pretend that the fabric of our common life has not been torn."[19] Any consideration of community life must include the practice of reconciliation with those from whom we are estranged, those with whom we disagree, and those whom we have injured or offended. Clearly, Anglicans, like other Christian bodies, have not always handled dissent or difference within their common life well. Even a cursory reading of the Tudor era in which the Anglican Church was established, with its stories of burnings, beheadings, and torture of those who dissented from the religious preferences of the ruler, attests to this. And yet our history can be instructive in its horror, for if Anglicans are often accused of being ambiguous and unclear in spelling out their doctrines, the reason for such hesitancy to define Christian truth too definitively often lies in our deep historical knowledge of what happens when one side or one group assumes the power to define that truth or prescribe Christian practice for all people and all time. After decades of bloodshed, vitriol, and bitter accusations among church and political leaders alike, Queen Elizabeth is famously quoted as having "no desire to make windows into men's souls." She thus set forth the hope of a measure of reasonable tolerance in the practice of religion, at least for the standards of that time, even though she herself was not always able to fulfill it.

In our own day, angry polemic combined with an exaggerated sense of certainty in defining Christian truth and practice has continued to create dissent and destroy trust among a number of the communities of the Episcopal Church. Some congregations have struggled to find ways of distancing themselves from communities with whose beliefs and practices they disagree, while remaining part of the larger Anglican Communion. At times the ideal of church unity upheld by the early apostles and bishops seems as elusive to us as it must have originally seemed to them. As early as the third century, Cyprian of Carthage asked in his treatise *On the Unity of the Church*, "Do you think that you can stand and live if you withdraw from the church, building for yourself other homes and a different dwelling?" Quoting the apostle Paul, he urged his congregations to end their schisms and live in unity, "forbearing one another in love, endeavoring to keep the unity of the Spirit in the bond of peace." For just as the Holy Spirit came as a dove, "a simple and joyous creature, not bitter with gall" and "remaining faithful to their mate and young throughout their lives," Cyprian believed "this is the simplicity that ought to be known in the Church, this is the charity that ought to be attained, that so the love of the brotherhood may imitate the doves, that their gentleness and meekness may be like the lambs and sheep." There is no place for venom and cruelty in the Christian community, Cyprian asserted, for "bitterness cannot consist and be associated with sweetness, darkness with light, rain with clearness, battle with peace, barrenness with fertility, drought with springs, storm with tranquility."[20]

It is perhaps in times and places such as these that the baptismal call to "seek and serve Christ in all persons, loving your neighbor as yourself" is most clarifying, refocusing the life of the community in the simplicity of charity for others, who are to be honored as Christ. This simplicity may require a shift in our priorities, in our way of "being church." It may require repentance and reconciliation among people who have been estranged. It may require repeated practice in the discipline of learning hospitality and openness to the "other" who challenges our comfortable sense of who God is and what faith in that God might entail.

On this challenging path of Christian unity, Benedict offers an insight as worthy of consideration now as it was when he first wrote his rule. In a chapter on mutual obedience, Benedict declares that if any member of the community discovers that another member is "angry or disturbed with them, however slightly, that member must, then and there without delay, fall down on the ground at the other's feet to make satisfaction, and lie there until the disturbance is calmed by a blessing." At first glance this practice seems from a distant place and time: when the members of my parish's Benedictine group read this chapter together, it was so far outside the scope of our experience that we chuckled at the thought of practicing such prostrations in our own parish. Yet as we considered the passage more thoughtfully, we grew to appreciate its simple wisdom in restoring and maintaining the unity of peace, regardless of who is right and who is wrong. "The question in the rule is who is offended and who is sorry, who is to apologize and who is to forgive," observes Joan Chittister in her commentary on the Rule. "Quickly. Immediately. Now."

How often do we wait for others to apologize first, to admit their fault, the members of the group asked themselves, or even to tell us why they are offended? How would our Christian communities be transformed if we addressed discord and "disturbance" quickly and directly, taking the initiative for forgiveness in love and humility, and waiting patiently for the blessing of the one who is offended? Chittister goes on to tell the Hasidic story of the rabbi of Sassov, who gave the last of his money to a "man of ill repute," who quickly went and squandered it all. When the rabbi's disciples berated him for his wastefulness, he answered them, "Shall I be more finicky than God, who gave it to me?" Thus what Benedictine spirituality can teach us about community life today, Chittister concludes, "is that we must all relate to one other knowing our own sinfulness and depending on the love we learn from one another."[21]

"See how they love one another!" marveled the opponents of the early Christians. In places where this radical hospitality and care is exercised today, there we will see conversion of life and growth in holiness. And there we will find Christians who are able to be mature members of the body of Christ, seeking and serving the Christ they see in others. In our final chapter we will consider some of the ways this service has taken form in the church throughout the centuries, as Christians have sought to bring about the justice and peace of the kingdom of God.

Anglican Voices on Community

Always keep God's peace and love among you, and when you have to seek guidance about your affairs, take great care to be of one mind. Live in mutual good-will also with Christ's other servants, and do not despise Christians who come to you for hospitality, but see that you welcome them, give them accommodation, and send them on their way with friendship and kindness.

—Last words of Cuthbert, bishop of Lindisfarne (687)

Early in September, a solicitation appeared in the Public papers, to the people of color to come forward and assist the distressed, perishing, and neglected sick [from yellow fever]; with a kind of assurance, that people of our color were not liable to take the infection. Upon which we and a few others met and consulted how to act on so truly alarming and melancholy an occasion. After some conversations, we found a freedom to go forth, confining in Him who can preserve in the midst of a burning fiery furnace, sensible that it was our duty to do all the good we could to our suffering fellow mortals. We set out to see where we could be useful. The first we visited was a man in Emsley's alley, who was dying, and his wife lay dead at the time in the house, there were none to assist but two poor helpless children. We administered what relief we could, and applied to the overseers of the poor to have the woman buried. We visited upwards of twenty families that day—they were scenes of woe indeed! The Lord was pleased to strengthen, and remove all fear from us, and disposed our hearts to be as useful as possible.

—Absalom Jones and Richard Allen, *A Narrative of the Proceedings of the Black People, during the Late Awful Calamity in Philadelphia, in the Year 1793* (1794)

The surest way to uphold or restore our endangered church will be for each of her anxious children, in his own place and station, to resign himself more thoroughly to his God and Savior in those duties, public and private, which are not immediately affected by the emergencies of the moment: the daily and hourly duties, I mean, of piety, purity, charity, justice.

—John Keble, "National Apostasy" (1833)

If there is anything in the teaching of the New Testament which is in the nature of a command, it is that you are obliged to take the sacrament, and you can't do it without going to church. I disliked very much their hymns, which I considered to be fifth-rate poems set to sixth-rate music. But as I went on I saw the great merit of it. I came up against different people of quite different outlooks and different education, and then gradually my conceit just began peeling off. I realized that the hymns (which were just sixth-rate music) were, nevertheless, being sung with devotion and benefit by an old saint in elastic-side boots in the opposite pew, and then you realize that you aren't fit to clean those boots. It gets you out of your solitary conceit.

—C. S. Lewis, "Answers to Questions on Christianity" (1944)[22]

God came into history to create a people who would change the world, who would make the world a place where every person knew that he or she was loved, was valued, had a contribution to make, and had just as much right to the riches of the world as every other person. That is what the church is all about, to bring into being that vision, that ideal community of love in which we all are equally valuable and in which we equally share. Every structure of life comes under the judgment of that vision: our politics, our economics, our education, our social structures. Even the church!

—Verna J. Dozier, *The Authority of the Laity* (1982)[23]

A friend of mine who is a hermit calls Vigils "the prayer office for pious insomniacs." On a more serious note, though, many religious people are wakened by the Spirit in the middle of the night in order to pray for someone in need. It is a common experience among Christians to discover that at the exact hour when someone needing to be commended to God was ministered to, a friend was raised from sleep on the other side of the globe. . . .

So I commend myself to God in prayer before I sleep. Something of our soul will remain linked to that warm darkness beyond its boundary, even in sleep. This dark love, more intimate than a mother's womb, nourishes, encourages, and guides us, enveloping us in its loving, wordless darkness. When we pay attention, and respond with wordless, loving prayer in the darkness of our souls, we know we are connected to divine life. When we commend our souls to God at night, we take this connection for granted. Awake or asleep, we live in the Lord.

—Suzanne Guthrie, *Praying the Hours* (2000)[23]

Love for God cannot be separated from love of neighbor. Jesus calls us to love God through our neighbor—by visiting prisoners, by hospitality to strangers, by actions that ostensibly give us no reward at the end of a long day's work. Jesus seems idealistic at best. When we look around and see others prospering through violence or greed, most of us pay little attention to God's love. How can we? After all, we live in a "real" world in which survival is paramount. Work with prisoners or those on death row may be typical of God's kind of love, which gravitates toward generosity and gift, but not for our kind of love that is seeking to survive in a violent world. Jesus knows our dilemma, but he does not let us off the hook. He still requires us to channel God's infinite generosity. Just as we cannot love God without loving our neighbor, we cannot worship in a church building without also ministering in a jail, hospital, or school.

God's love always points toward the capacity to love outside of self-interest. When it came to heaven, Jesus was no realist—if by realism we mean self-interest. This was his genius. Perhaps the greatest lesson in this for us is to learn that we must prepare to love as God loves—through random acts of kindness. We prepare through our daily prayers. We prepare through the butterflies in our stomach when we make our first volunteer visit in a jail. This kind of preparation hones our skills of navigation as we make our way toward heaven—toward the real heaven, not just our own narcissistic version of heaven. We must practice heaven. In so doing, we catch glimpses of God's idea of what's real because we are increasing our attention span to see beyond the ordinary.

—Michael Battle, "A Strange Route to Heaven" (2007)[24]

Questions for Reflection and Discussion

1. Where have you experienced Christian community? How would you describe the most important aspects of community life for you? When have you needed a Christian community but been unable to find it?

2. What is your experience of monastic communities or rules of life? Do you have a rule of life? What does it include?

3. In the quotation immediately preceding these questions, Michael Battle describes a few of the ways we "prepare to love as God loves": acts of kindness to others, daily prayers, visiting those in prison. What are some of the ways you practice loving others as God loves them? How do you "practice heaven" by your care for others?

Practicing Heaven

Will you strive for justice and peace among all people, and respect the dignity of every human being? (BCP 305)

It was a fine, bright spring afternoon. We heard the fire engines and rushed into the square to see what was going on. We saw the smoke pouring out of the building. We got there just as they started to jump. I shall never forget the frozen horror which came over us as we stood with our hands on our throats watching that horrible sight, knowing that there was no help. They came down in twos and threes, jumping together in a kind of desperate hope. The life nets were broken. The firemen kept shouting for them not to jump. But they had no choice; the flames were right behind them for by this time the fire was far gone.

Out of that terrible episode came a self-examination of stricken conscience in which the people of this state saw for the first time the individual worth and value of each of those 146 people who fell or were burned in that great fire. And we saw, too, the great human value of every individual who was injured in an accident by a machine.

There was a stricken conscience of public guilt and we all felt that we had been wrong, that something was wrong with that building which we had accepted or the tragedy never would have happened. Moved by this sense of stricken guilt, we banded ourselves together to find a way by law to prevent this kind of disaster.[1]

Frances Perkins was forever changed by the burning of the Triangle Shirtwaist Factory in New York, where she saw working men, women, and girls who had been locked into the eighth, ninth, and tenth stories of a building with inadequate fire escapes jumping to their deaths that March afternoon. The tragedy confirmed the compelling need for safeguards and laws that would protect workers, and set her on a lifelong path of fighting for just wages and safe conditions for working people. Later, as secretary of labor in the administration of Franklin Delano Roosevelt, Perkins would remark that "the Triangle fire was the first day of the New Deal."[2] "We had in the election of Franklin Roosevelt the beginning of what has come to be called a New Deal for the United States," she wrote. "But it was based really upon the experiences that we had had in New York State and upon the sacrifices of those who, we faithfully remember with affection and respect, died in that terrible fire on March 25, 1911. They did not die in vain and we will never forget them."[3]

Like Frances Perkins, many of the people who are remembered in the Episcopal Church for their prophetic witness in areas of social justice and peace heard that baptismal call to "strive for justice and peace" and "respect the dignity of every human being" after seeing the results of injustice, violence, and inhumanity firsthand. At some point the awareness of systemic inequalities or societal structures that deny opportunities and even health to individuals becomes acute, and compels us to act. While this question in the Baptismal Covenant comes last in the series and might therefore seem less important than the study of Scripture and theology, the practice of prayer, and life in community, our efforts to bring about a more just world are our witness to a biblically and theologically informed faith. "Christian social witness is not merely a footnote to these foundations of our faith," Harold T. Lewis writes, "but is an outgrowth of them. It is faith in action. It is what we do as a consequence of what we believe."[4]

Thus the verbs used in this question of the Baptismal Covenant are strong and active, not passive or merely reflective. Our efforts in striving for justice encompass a breadth of community beyond our local connections, beyond the Christian church, to include "all people" and "every human being." These are sweeping, powerful demands for action that require us to live with integrity what we say we believe in our hearts. This question of the Baptismal Covenant leads us with urgency to ask how we can practice our faith in action as well as word. "How can I work for justice?" asks Marianne Micks in her book on the Nicene Creed. "How can I best contribute to peace? Believing and doing go hand in hand."[5]

What we believe to be true about the nature and character of God will profoundly influence how we respond to this baptismal question. What does it mean to believe that God is a God of justice? Words for "justice" in Hebrew and Greek appear more than one thousand times in Scripture, and God is so closely identified with justice that we might say it is inherently part of God's character. The law codes of the Hebrew scriptures make it clear that God's justice has implications for the way we live in human community, for we are to be equally concerned with right dealings with others. "You shall not render an unjust judgment," the Hebrew people are instructed in the law. "You shall not be partial to the poor or defer to the great: with justice you shall judge your neighbor" (Lev. 19:15). The prophet Isaiah spoke the word of the Lord instructing the people of Israel how to practice their faith in caring for one another, saying, "Is not this the fast that I choose: to loose the bonds of injustice, to undo the thongs of the yoke, to let the oppressed go free, and to break every yoke? Is it not to share your bread with the hungry, and bring the homeless poor into your house; when you see the naked, to cover them, and not to hide yourself from your own kin?" (Isa. 58:6–7). Among the most widely known passages in the Bible is this summary from the prophet Micah: "What does the Lord require of you but to do justice, and to love kindness, and to walk humbly with your God?" (Mic. 6:8). In these and many other passages in the Hebrew scriptures, we hear justice to mean the restoration of right judgment and equity, peace and harmony, to our common life.

Furthermore, the quest for justice often focuses on economic disparities and the misuse of power. "God's justice applies to every form of abuse of power, unjust economic distribution, or violation of human rights present in society," writes the theologian C. René Padilla. "God's justice embraces every human relationship and seeks to abolish every manifestation of injustice."[6] Jesus echoed this passion for just dealings in human societies in his inaugural address to the people of his synagogue in Nazareth, when he announced that he had come to fulfill the words of the prophet Isaiah promising "good news to the poor," as well as release to the captives, restoration of sight to the blind, and freedom for the oppressed (Luke 4:18–19). Throughout his life and teachings, Jesus affirmed that God is concerned not just with our spiritual lives, but with our bodily cares, our material well-being, our relationships with one another. "The church is called to witness to the Incarnate Christ in all the conditions of human existence," notes theologian James Griffiss, "including politics and economics, war and peace, literature and the arts, and in the natural world we inhabit."[7] In other words, the good news of the gospel is a message from which justice is inseparable.

How each of us will come to express the justice of God in our lives and world will vary according to circumstances and time, personality and culture. Indeed, social customs and ways of being change over time, and how we answer this question of the covenant will need to be reexamined and reevaluated in the light of the particular needs of a changing society. The Episcopal Church has been challenged by new and urgent social problems in recent decades, from racism to the environment, from the rights of women and gay and lesbian people to immigration reform, from questions of war and peace to economic and global concerns for justice. While examples of individual and communal prophetic Christian witness regarding these issues abound among Anglicans, they are far too numerous, complex, and varied to be discussed adequately in this chapter. Here we will provide only a brief hearing of some of the voices that have influenced the human social justice conversation through the centuries, in an effort to see how Anglicans have attempted to live out their faith in a God who enters our world to redeem our sufferings, and who leads us both to rethink and act upon the patterns of inequity and prejudice that permeate human societies. By listening to their voices in this way, we will discern some the spiritual practices that have supported and made possible the many different social justice ministries and prophetic witness of Anglicans throughout the centuries.

ENDING SLAVERY

It is ironic that the arrival of Augustine of Canterbury in the British Isles was due to the brisk trade in English slaves in Roman Britain. The historian Bede records the story of Gregory the Great seeing a number of English boys awaiting sale at the market in Rome, and asking the pope to send him and other preachers of the gospel to Britain as missionaries. His pleas were not granted, but as soon as Gregory succeeded to the papacy himself, Bede tells us, "he put in hand this long cherished project and sent other missionaries in his place, assisting their work by his own prayers and encouragement."[8]

As Christianity continued to expand among the tribes of Anglo-Saxon England, a number of church leaders joined with those political rulers of like mind in attempting to end the sale of human beings both at home and abroad. The seventh-century bishop Aidan, for example—whose holiness of life, we are told, prompted kings and earls to shower him with gifts—spent nearly all his wealth in ransoming those who had been sold into slavery, and kings like Alfred the Great and William the Conquerer passed laws against the selling of slaves, especially out of the country. Bishops encouraged their people to give slaves their freedom, and they set an example by baptizing and freeing the slaves who came into their possession by gift. "They were eminently successful with men who were on the point of death," one historian wryly noted, "for though the Anglo-Saxon, when in good health, was very reluctant to manumit a slave, he was willing to practise the posthumous charity of freeing him by his will."[9] Bishops also had some success in limiting the power owners held over their slaves by upholding the Lord's Day as one on which no one worked, and exhorting their congregations to allow slaves to accumulate a small measure of property and material goods. Despite all these efforts, however, the slave trade in the British Isles continued in those border places where there were tribes at war and defeated soldiers were readily available for sale, or where poverty was so intense that slavery seemed the only option for parents who could not feed their children, or for gamblers or debtors who failed to pay off their debts.

Merchants of the seaside town of Bristol were singled out for the particularly egregious nature of its slave trade. "The people of this town," William of Malmesbury records in his *Chronicle of the Kings of England*,

> had a most odious and inveterate custom, which they derived from their ancestors, of buying men and women in all parts of England, and exporting them to Ireland for the sake of gain. The young women they commonly got with child, and carried them to market in their pregnancy that they might bring a better price. You might have seen with sorrow long ranks of young persons of both sexes and of the greatest beauty tied with ropes and daily exposed for sale.

Wulftan, the eleventh-century bishop of Worcester, was horrified at such practices, and he repeatedly visited Bristol to preach against the slave trade, often remaining two months at a time. His words eventually dissuaded those who continued the practice and the traders finally abandoned it. The Archbishop of Canterbury of the time, Lanfranc, likewise brought pressure to bear on William the Conqueror to end the slave trade to Ireland, despite the lucrative tolls it brought into his kingdom, and in 1102 the Council of Westminster outlawed it in England.

Slavery would once again become a virulent force in the seventeenth century, however, as markets for African slaves were developed by the European and British colonial powers. Once again it would take a combination of intense and long-term efforts by religious and political leaders and socially conscious individuals such as John Newton, William Wilberforce, and Lord Shaftsbury to outlaw the slave trade in England. Before he became a Christian, Anglican clergyman, and outspoken abolitionist, John Newton was the captain of a slave-trading ship on the western coast of Africa. In 1788 he wrote a pamphlet to aid the efforts of William Wilberforce in Parliament to pass legislation to end the slave trade. In *Thoughts Upon the African Slave Trade*, Newton wrote that because

of his familiarity with and participation in the slave trade, he felt
bound by a guilty conscience to speak out:

> Silence, at such a time, and on such an occasion, would, in me,
> be criminal. If my testimony should not be necessary, or service-
> able, yet, perhaps, I am bound, in conscience, to take shame to
> myself for a public confession, which, however sincere, comes
> too late to prevent, or repair, the misery and mischief to which
> I have, formerly, been accessory. I hope it will always be a sub-
> ject of humiliating reflection to me, that I was, once, an active
> instrument, in a business at which my heart now shudders.

While it is not an easy matter to reflect "with coolness upon this
business," Newton observed, his experience of seeing the "horrid
features of the African Trade" left an indelible mark on his soul and
remained a formative power in his life and ministry. As a slave-ship
captain he knew the terrible effect of having "unlimited power,
instigated by revenge" of one human being over another. It is a
terrible thing, he wrote, when "the heart, by a long familiarity with
the sufferings of Slaves, is become callous, and insensible to the
pleadings of humanity."

Newton's words to the hymn "Amazing Grace" have for generations since expressed the personal, brokenhearted knowledge of
human sin and suffering as well as a profound gratitude for the
merciful salvation of a loving God. Although in its origins the
hymn was not explicitly linked to Newton's repentance for his
participation in the slave trade, it expressed a contrition and awareness of the need for compassion that later would be joined to the
abolitionist movement. Quoting it in her 1852 antislavery novel
Uncle Tom's Cabin, Harriet Beecher Stowe added a new verse taken
from an African-American spiritual: "When we've been there ten
thousand years,/ Bright shining as the sun,/ We've no less days to
sing God's praise/ Than when we'd first begun."

As a member of the British Parliament, and with the vigorous support of a group of evangelical Anglicans known as the Clapham Sect,
William Wilberforce drew upon the increasingly widespread public
awareness of the need to end the British slave trade, which he called

in his *Appeal to the Religion, Justice, and Humanity of the Inhabitants of the British Empire, in Behalf of the Negro Slaves in the West Indies* "a system of the grossest injustice, of the most heathenish irreligion and immorality, of the most unprecedented degradation, and unrelenting cruelty." While other abolitionists focused more on the particulars of "the great and numerous evils" of the slave trade, Wilberforce wanted to pass legislation outlawing the system of human ownership entirely. "When the public attention has been attracted to this subject," he wrote, "it has been unadvisedly turned to particular instances of cruelty, rather than to the system in general, and to those essential and incurable vices which will invariably exist wherever the power of man over man is unlimited." Wilberforce's efforts finally brought about the Slave Trade Act of 1807, banning the importation of African slaves into British colonies, and the Slavery Abolition Act of 1833 ending slavery in the British empire, though it continued in the United States until the Emancipation Proclamation of 1863.

In a nineteenth-century America deeply divided over the institution of slavery, prophetic voices were heard from people of many colors and races, social classes and political persuasions. Former slaves who spoke of their life in slavery and in a profoundly racist America remain particularly powerful for the church today. In the Episcopal Church calendar, we remember Frederick Douglass, Richard Allen, and Absalom Jones, freed slaves who were active abolitionists—Jones and Allen as priests and preachers in the African Methodist Episcopal Church, Douglass as a writer, journalist, and orator in the antislavery movement. Giving voice to those who had experienced slavery firsthand was an important part of dismantling the institution of slavery and establishing new values and ways of seeing people of different races. Freed African-Americans had to begin the process of reconciliation with the past and to learn how to live in a still racially divided society. Speaking the truth was a first step in this process. "The real feelings and opinions of the slaves were not much known or respected by their masters," wrote Frederick Douglass in his autobiography. "The distance between the two was too great to admit of such knowledge."

Douglass goes on to tell the story of a slave who met a white man on the road, and answered an honest "no" to the white man's

casual inquiry of whether his master treated him well. The slave
thought no more about the conversation until some two or three
weeks later, when he was chained and handcuffed and sold to a
Georgia trader for having spoken the truth to a man who turned
out to have been his master: "Thus, without a moment's warn-
ing, he was snatched away, and forever sundered from his family
and friends by a hand as unrelenting as that of death." Douglass
observed that "this was the penalty of telling the simple truth, in
answer to a series of plain questions":

> It was partly in consequence of such facts, that slaves, when
> inquired of as to their condition and the character of their mas-
> ters, would almost invariably say that they were contented and
> their masters kind. Slaveholders are known to have sent spies
> among their slaves to ascertain, if possible, their views and feel-
> ings in regard to their condition; hence the maxim established
> among them, that "a still tongue makes a wise head." They
> would suppress the truth rather than take the consequences for
> telling it, and in so doing they prove themselves a part of the
> human family. I was frequently asked if I had a kind master, and
> I do not remember ever to have given a negative reply. I did not
> consider myself as uttering that which was strictly untrue, for I
> always measured the kindness of my master by the standard of
> kindness set up by the slaveholders around us.[10]

Sojourner Truth, who fled slavery with the help of Quaker
friends, likewise became a strong voice speaking the truth about the
evils of slavery. After twenty-eight years in slavery, being sold from
household to household in New York, Isabella (as she was known
then) obtained her freedom and joined the Mother Zion African
Methodist Episcopal Church, becoming a street-corner evangelist
and advocate for homeless women. When at age forty-six she dis-
cerned a call to be a traveling preacher, she set out for New England.
On the way she stopped for water at a Quaker farm, and a woman
there asked her name. "My name is Sojourner," she replied. When
the woman asked what was her last name, all the last names—the
names of her masters—that she had been given in her life came into

her mind. All of them she rejected: "The only master I have now is God, and His name is Truth." For Sojourner Truth, as for all of these prophets of justice, speaking the truth in all places, even when that truth is not welcome or cannot be heard, is a foundational spiritual discipline for an authentic Christian social witness.

EQUALITY IN COMMUNITY

Sojourner Truth is commemorated on the same feast day as Harriet Tubman, an African-American slave who escaped into Canada and was known as the "Moses of her People" during her years of helping over three hundred slaves flee servitude in Maryland through the hidden network of safe houses known as the Underground Railroad. Tubman later spoke of her sense of calling to this work when she experienced her first exhilarating moments of freedom: "I looked at my hands, to see if I was the same person now I was free. There was such a glory over everything, the sun came like gold through the trees, and over the fields, and I felt like I was in heaven. I had crossed the line of which I had so long been dreaming." Her exultation was immediately tempered by the realization that personal freedom alone was not enough, Tubman saw she must also bring her family and fellow slaves into freedom with her, and create a home in this new world:

> I was free; but there was no one to welcome me to the land of freedom, I was a stranger in a strange land, and my home after all was down in the old cabin quarter, with the old folks, and my brothers and sisters. But to this solemn resolution I came: I was free, and they should be free also; I would make a home for them in the North, and the Lord helping me, I would bring them all there. Oh, how I prayed then, lying all alone on the cold, damp ground; "Oh, dear Lord," I said, "I ain't got no friend but you. Come to my help, Lord, for I'm in trouble!"[11]

Tubman's prayer has no doubt been echoed by anyone who has ever spoken an unwelcome truth, who has ever stood for a moral cause or principle that went against the prevailing norm, who has ever crossed the dividing line into a community where difference is not valued. Race and economic status have long been among those lines drawn in human societies, but the divisions are also keenly felt by women who seek to enter professions previously reserved to men, by pacifists who enter the political fray in times of war, and by theologians and economists who question the equity and morality of our economic structures. It is often much easier to speak one's truth in the safety of one's family or friends; confronting those who hold opposing views or who are actively working against one's cause or values can have painful and long-lasting consequences.

Florence Li Tim-Oi knew those consequences, when she was ordained as the first woman priest in the Anglican Communion. At the time of her birth in 1907, a bowl of ash was often at hand during the birth of a child in order to smother unwanted newborn girls. Her father chose to name her Tim-Oi ("Much Beloved"), so she would know that far from being a disappointment to him, she was very much wanted. When Tim-Oi became a Christian, she took the baptismal name Florence, after Florence Nightingale, who was best known for her nursing skills but was also a woman who experienced a call to priesthood but was denied it. After attending seminary and serving for two years at a parish in the absence of a priest in Macau, Florence Tim-Oi was ordained in 1944 by Bishop Ronald Hall of Hong Kong, who believed it was clear that God had already given her the gift of priesthood. In a letter to Florence written fifty years later by that bishop's son, Christopher Hall, he asks:

> Did my father tell you that he was tempted to give you a new name—Cornelia? He recognised, even if you did not, that to ordain a woman was equivalent to Peter baptising the gentile Cornelius—quite contrary to the then understanding of God's will. Peter had been shown that, contrary to Jewish belief, gentiles were not unclean—and neither are women. What mattered to my father, as mattered to Peter, was that God had already given to you the gift of priesthood, which for three years you had been licensed to exercise, and your ministry had been manifestly blessed. Who was he to deny what God had already done?[12]

Pressure from the Anglican bishops opposed to her ordination led Florence to give up her license to practice as a priest in order to protect Bishop Hall from censure, but she did not resign her holy orders. She was placed in charge of a parish near Vietnam, where she started a large maternity hospital in which newborn girls were cherished rather than smothered at birth. Life under the Maoist leaders involved severe suffering for Florence and many other Christians in China; the practice of their religion was banned and the Red Guards forced her to cut up her priestly vestments with scissors. She emerged from these years stronger and more committed to her faith, and Christopher Hall remarked that what was true of his father was equally true of Florence: "She showed us how the Christ she talked about is living now."

In 1989, three years before her death in 1992, Florence Li Tim-Oi joined Carter Heyward, one of the first women priests ordained in the Episcopal Church, at the altar to celebrate the eucharist at the consecration of the suffragan bishop of Massachusetts, Barbara Harris. "A woman had become a bishop," one historian observed, "and the episcopacy had been transformed: no longer a male preserve, it had become an image of human leadership within a community of diverse men and women united in Christ's service."[13]

Like Ronald Hall, another bishop also faced controversy and censure for the stand that he took for an issue of social justice, though in a different time and place. Paul Jones, the bishop of Utah in the years leading up to World War I, was forced to resign his post because of his opposition to the war. Though he believed that "German brutality and aggression must be stopped," Jones told the House of Bishops, and though like other loyal citizens was willing "to give my life and what I possess to bring that about," he disagreed as to the method of bringing about in the world "a sound and lasting peace."

> We all feel that war is wrong, evil, and undesirable. Many even feel that war is unchristian but unavoidable as the world is now constituted, and that the present situation forces us to use it. Some contend that this is a righteous war, and that we must all fight the devil with fire, even at the danger of being scorched,

or all the ideals which we hold dear will go by the board, and therefore we are solemnly, sadly, and earnestly taking that way.

Jones declared that while he agreed with the need to oppose evil in the world, he had nevertheless "been led to feel that war is entirely incompatible with the Christian profession" and that the only way in which the gospel will transform the world is to hold up the way of the cross, as "the one way our Lord has given us for overcoming the world."

> Prayer is, I believe, the best test of the whole matter. If it is right and our honest duty to fight the war to a finish, then we should use the Church's great weapon of prayer to that end; but the most ardent Christian supporter of the war, though he may use general terms, revolts against praying that our every bullet may find its mark, or that our embargoes may bring starvation to every German home. We know that those things would bring the war to a speedy, triumphant close, but the Church cannot pray that way. And a purpose that you cannot pray for is a poor one for Christians to be engaged in.[14]

Many Episcopalians agreed with Jones but many did not; as in most wars, the church was torn. Bishop Jones agreed to resign his position as a diocesan bishop but continued to work for peace in the world. As part of his commitment, Jones helped to establish the Episcopal Pacifist Fellowship, now the Episcopal Peace Fellowship, a national network providing education and resources leading toward a more just and peaceful world through local community efforts. Jones continued his own mission to "do justice, dismantle violence, and strive to be peace makers"[15] to the end of his life in 1941, helping to resettle Jews and other refugees from the Nazi regime in Germany during World War II and advocating a greater understanding between the nations of Japan and the United States as a means of avoiding war. "The day will come when, like slavery which was once held in good repute, war will be looked upon as thoroughly un-Christian," Jones optimistically believed. "Only when Christian men and women and churches will be brave enough to stand openly for the full truth that their consciences are beginning to recognize, will the terrible anachronism of war . . . be done away."[16]

A MORAL ECONOMY

"Central to what Christian theology sets before us is mutuality," Archbishop Rowan Williams noted in his recent address to the Trinity Institute in New York City on the economy. "What affects one affects all, for good and ill, since both suffering and flourishing belong to the entire organism, not to any individual or purely local grouping." In this understanding of the nature of human communities on both a local and a global scale, "each person is both needy and needed, both dependent on others and endowed with gifts for others." In other words, Archbishop Williams continued, "each believer is called to see himself or herself as equally helpless alone and gifted in relationship":

> This is where we start in addressing the world of economics from a Christian standpoint. No process whose goal is the limited or exclusive security of an individual or an interest group or even a national community alone can be regarded as unequivocally good in Christian terms because of the underlying aspiration to a state of security in isolation. If my well-being is inseparable in God's community from the well-being of all others, a global economic ethic in which the indefinitely continuing poverty or disadvantage of some is taken for granted has to be decisively left behind.[17]

It is this sense of mutuality and "indwelling" that is the foundation for a Christian attitude toward the economic structures that determine our material well-being in human societies. While some in Christian history have objected to the church's interference in economic or political matters, Jesus himself taught that wealth and work are intimately connected to our spiritual lives; as aspects of our just dealings with one another, they also matter to a God who loves justice. We are all part of one body, inseparably connected within the community of God, and therefore how we conduct our relationships with money and time, employers and employees, the wealthy and the poor, is crucial to the Christian life.

A passion for upholding the common good and caring for those in need inspired many of the writings and sermons of the apostolic teachers and bishops of the early church. While the first Christian communities held property in common, that ideal seems to have been quickly lost as the church expanded into other countries within the Roman empire and grew in size, wealth, and influence. Yet improving the lot of the poor remained a powerful tenet of the early church's life. In the fourth century Basil the Great was particularly forceful in his desire to encourage the formation of a society in which the needs of all are provided for: "While we try to amass wealth, make piles of money, get hold of the land as our real property, overtop one another in riches," he preached, "we have palpably cast off justice, and lost the common good. I should like to know how any man can be just, who is deliberately aiming to get out of someone else what he wants for himself." Basil and many other church leaders struggled with the inequality of the distribution of goods and the social stratifications engendered by wealth and poverty, issues of common life and social justice that would remain unresolved in the centuries to come.

Over the centuries many Anglicans have spoken out about the church's call to care for the poor. "In Christ we are all of one degree, without respect of persons," wrote William Tyndale in 1528, and although our hearts are open to all, because our resources are limited and our "ability of goods extendeth not so far," our responsibility for material care lies first with providing for our own household. His scheme is both pragmatic and bold: "When you have done your duty to your household, and yet have further abundance of the blessing of God, you owe that to the poor that cannot labor, or would labor and can get no work, and are destitute of friends; to the poor, I mean, whom you know, to those of your own parish." The responsibility for the welfare of others, moreover, extends even further beyond the local community: if all your neighbors have been cared for and you still have "superfluity," then you are a debtor to those even "a thousand miles off." Unlike many Christians of his own day, Tyndale would even extend the community of Christian concern to the "infidels" of other lands and nations, as long as the funds were not used in ways to "blaspheme Christ."[18]

Three centuries later F. D. Maurice would also emphasize the theme of Christian responsibility for the common good in his writings on the kingdom of God. "Christ came to establish a kingdom, not to proclaim a set of opinions," he wrote. "Every man entering this kingdom becomes interested in all its relations, members, circumstances; he cannot separate himself in any wise from them." Furthermore, while we understand ourselves to be members of a great company of the faithful in all times and places, the Christian faith can only be acted upon in the local circumstances in which Christians live. We are citizens of the world, Maurice believed, but therefore also citizens of a particular country, and must involve ourselves in "everything which affects its weal or woe, everything which concerns the bodily or the external, as well as the spiritual condition of its inhabitants."[19]

One of the avenues through which Maurice's teachings reached the Episcopal Church was the preaching of Phillips Brooks, renowned minister of Trinity Church, Copley Square, in Boston. The compassionate theology of Brooks and Maurice restated the church's understanding of God in terms of a loving and gracious Savior intimately involved in the world, rather than a distant God of harsh and eternal judgment, and they spoke of a "wideness in God's mercy" that encompassed people of all nations, races, and walks of life. Through their teaching, alongside that of many other Broad Church theologians and pastors of the day, Gilded Age Americans who witnessed the severe social dislocations and inequality brought about by rapid industrialization of the northern states in the late nineteenth century were given a vision and call to work for the alleviation of suffering and the rights of the working poor.

One of the parishioners who heard and received the message of Phillips Brooks was the mother of Vida Dutton Scudder. "The gracious teaching of Phillips Brooks, and the thought of F. D. Maurice, so dear to my mother, had saved me," Scudder would later recall. "The stern terrors of Calvinism, and the sentimental revivalist ardors into which it rose—or sank—at times, both passed me by."[20] Scudder would go on to study at Smith College and Oxford, where she was deeply affected by the socialist critique of industrial capitalism and her visits to the slums of London's East End. Inspired by a visit to Toynbee Hall, Scudder joined with other Smith graduates in opening a similar settlement house in New York in 1889, in which privileged, educated women lived as neighbors among the poor. Both University Settlement House on Rivington Street and Hull House, the settlement house established by Jane Addams in Chicago, nurtured the early seeds of Progressive Era reforms. The young women who lived and volunteered at the settlement houses—among whom was Frances Perkins—helped to improve the working and living conditions of immigrants and the urban poor.

Many of the settlement workers and college graduates were Episcopalians, and of these a large number joined a prayer association for women founded in 1884 called the Society of the Companions of the Holy Cross (SCHC). The SCHC was committed to intercessory prayer, with a broad concern for social welfare. In its Companion Conference of 1909, participants were asked three questions: "What can the church do to aid social justice? What can the SCHC do? and What is the duty of the individual Companion in this regard?" Over the decades since, the SCHC has sought to educate and support its companions in their efforts to "aid social justice" in a broad variety of arenas, from racial justice and child labor laws to nonviolent settlements of international conflicts and the alleviation of world hunger. In newsletters, retreats, and conferences, through their prayer and study SCHC members were asked to face what founder Emily Morgan called "the great democracy of suffering." If their Christian faith was not to "end in a mere vapor of talk," Morgan wrote, the companions must make a "practical application of our commitment to social justice" through an awareness of the world's suffering, which is the "experience that makes the whole world kin."[21] One historian summarized the "real ministry" of the companions to the intellectual, spiritual, and moral life of the church as a "commitment to reality-based self-education for Christians—learning to distinguish between overt piety and theological insight."[22] This focus on bringing to the church's care the real situation of real people in the world was cited by the national church staff for industrial relations in 1930, when it praised the SCHC for all it had done "to awaken the Church to its responsibility in the vast field of industrial and labor relations," and for continuing "to help in the building up of a consciousness of the social demands on the Church and its stewardship of the faith and the Gospel of Christ."[23]

Vida Scudder was a leading member of the SCHC, and served for thirty-five years as their Companion in Charge of Probationers, who were aspirants to the Society. In one of her letters, printed in the 1925 Companion Conference Report, she defined the companions as "a group living under definite vows, strengthened by a corporate prayer life, and aiming to specialize in spiritual goals." Their vows were supported through prayer, study, intercession, and a daily discipline, similar to the vows taken by men and women in religious orders, although they spent their lives not in monastic enclosure but in the world. For Scudder, her vows encompassed a forty-year teaching career at Wellesley College and her sometimes radical writing and activism for the social welfare of all. "The responsibility for social intercession is not satisfied by vague aspiration, 'Thy Kingdom Come,'" she wrote in her essay "Social Problems Facing the Church," in which she urges the church to learn how to use the "prayer of power" for the common good:

> That petition, to be sure, covers all our desires; but if we pray specifically for the recovery to health of a beloved friend, for example, we should be equally specific in our prayers for the health of the body politic. Now we can not be specific unless we have some conviction and some intelligence. There is a type of purely formal prayer; not wholly useless, we hope. But most Christian people have some little experience at least of another kind of prayer, the prayer of power. That kind of a prayer must be enlightened; it must be lit at the torch of knowledge. The chief reason why all Christian people should be making themselves intelligent about the great issues of the day, is that they may learn to pray with fervor and to use the prayer of power.

Even if Christians are unsure how to act in practical and political ways for social justice, they need to cultivate what Scudder calls their "social imagination." Both study and prayer are necessary, if preliminary, steps in educating oneself about the sufferings and life conditions of others. Ultimately they will bring a deeper sense of connection to and responsibility for others, and a "sure release from bewildered and unworthy private-mindedness."

Many members of the Companions of the Society of the Holy Cross not only became well-informed and active in their prayer, but also played leading roles in the various turn-of-the-century reform movements based on what they had learned and seen with their own eyes. In the midst of a violent labor dispute between mill owners and workers in Lawrence, Massachusetts, for example, Scudder spoke at a public meeting at the invitation of the strike committee. Her speech supporting the strikers was later published, and nearly cost her her teaching position at Wellesley:

> I would rather never again wear a thread of woolen than know my garments had been woven at the cost of such misery as I have seen and known past the shadow of a doubt to have existed in this town. . . . If the wages are of necessity below the standard to maintain man and woman in decency and in health, then the woolen industry has not a present right to exist in Massachusetts.[24]

We hear in her speech echoes of the story of the silk dress Frances Perkins saw in a New York store window, in which she reminds us that workers deserve to earn a living wage, and the cost of making, selling, and purchasing cheap clothing created in sweatshops that reduce people to abject poverty is too high for a moral society to pay.

RESPECTING DIFFERENCE

While Christians have addressed issues of economic, political, and social justice in an infinite variety of ways, at the heart of any vision of a just world is the baptismal call to "respect the dignity of every human being." The Christian's fundamental belief in the holiness of each individual as created in the image of God calls the church to uphold the dignity of that individual, regardless of nationality or race, economic status or social class, religious creed or political stance. Learning to affirm the dignity of those very different from ourselves requires practice, for we must develop eyes to see and ears to hear in order to be open to the Christ present in others. We are helped in this process by the disciplines of prayer and worship that provide experience of the God who hears our prayers in many languages, and the practice of deep listening to our fears and biases, our hopes and needs, as well as to the truth of others' faith and experience of God—especially when it is markedly different from our own.

"God invites his people to enjoy diversity," states the 1998 summary of the work of the Inter-Anglican Theological and Doctrinal Commission known as *The Virginia Report*. This diversity of gifts and persons must be celebrated not in isolation, but within the context of the "mutuality and interdependence of each member," so that "the gifts of all contribute to the building up of the community and the fulfillment of its calling." And this unity of the body of Christ, the report affirms, is most richly experienced in the service of Holy Eucharist, which is the source of our call to address injustice and restore peace in our world:

> All injustice, racism, separation and denial of freedom are radically challenged when Christians share in the body and blood of Christ. Through the eucharist the grace of God penetrates, restores and renews human personality and dignity. The eucharist involves believers in the central event of the world's history, the passion, death and resurrection of Christ, and sends them into the world in peace to love and serve the Lord.[25]

Anglicans, like other denominations, have a mixed record when it comes to celebrating diversity and helping to restore "human personality and dignity." Occasions of true generosity and openness to seeing Christ in "the other" abound in the stories that comprise the history of our church; we have cause to celebrate the end of slavery, the increasing equality among races and genders, and the growing awareness of our global interdependence, as witnessed by our adoption of the United Nations' Millennium Development Goals. Yet we have our failures, too, such as those times we have imposed our culture and religious assumptions on those of other countries or races, or turned a blind eye to the genocide taking place in the world, or shirked our responsibilities on behalf of the poor and vulnerable.

Made up of churches from many nations and peoples, the global Anglican Communion provides ample opportunities to experience the challenges of abiding in unity amid diversity. While we are united by our shared theological and liturgical expressions as well as our common prayer, our communion with one another can only be sustained by the spiritual disciplines and practices of our long Christian tradition. John Mogabgab of *Weavings* sums up these practices well when he proposes they include "deep listening to God and one another, open and honest questions, authenticity in faith and life and belief that together we can stay in uncomfortable places long enough and attentively enough to be found by a truth larger than any we might discover on our own."[26] This confidence in the value of common wisdom, common exploration in discovering the God who unites us all, must be marked by a deep and generous conversation that truly welcomes the distinctive voices of all the people of God and believes that each should—indeed, must—be heard in order for the body to be whole and sound and to grow into maturity in Christ.

Anglicans struggle to find ways to practice listening to the many different voices that speak to our common life, and the fruits of that struggle can be seen in the changing face of Anglicanism in the twenty-first century. Divisions and dissension continue to thwart our hope of shared communion. Yet we continue in faith because every celebration of baptism and eucharist we are reminded we are in fact one body, with many members. We hold one faith, expressed in many different languages and images. We celebrate one baptism, which unites us to one another and to the one Triune God who created and loves us all.

ANGLICAN VOICES ON JUSTICE

So natural is the union of religion with justice, that we may boldly deem there is neither, where both are not. For how should they be unfeignedly just, whom religion doth not cause to be such; or they religious, which are not found such by the proof of their just actions?

—Richard Hooker, *Of the Laws of Ecclesiastical Polity* V.1.2
(1597)

God forbid that I should commend to your confidence that thin and sickly caricature of Catholicity which would bring men into one Church by bidding them first divest themselves of whatever is especially characteristic of their present and past belongings! That sort of thing is sometimes commended to us under the name of "unsectarian religion," and a very insipid nostrum it is. I distrust the forestry which under the pretext of unifying the trees of the wood begins by commanding the birch to denude itself of its peculiar bark, the oak to cast away its distinctive leaf, and the cedar to shed its cones. What should we have left but a totally uninteresting collection of bare poles?

—William Reed Huntington, "Whole Church: A Plea for
the Four Temperaments" (1895)

No positive good can be done by force; that is true. But evil can be checked and held back by force, and it is precisely for this that we may be called upon to use it. If it be so, let us do it in calm but unshakable resolution, trying, in spite of all the agony, to bear no ill-will to those whom we must resist, seeking to inflict no more suffering than is inevitably involved in the resistance that we must offer, bearing with patient courage the suffering that comes to ourselves. And while we do our utmost to secure the triumph of right as it has been given us to see the right, let us steadily look beyond the conflict to the restoration of peace, and dedicate ourselves to the creation of a world order which shall be fair to the generations yet unborn.

—William Temple, radio broadcast (1939)[27]

Prayer in some mysterious way we cannot see, has the effect of releasing the omnipotence of God upon the world. This is what

St. Thomas Aquinas meant by his great definition of prayer—
"Prayer is the means God wills us to use in order that we might
obtain the blessings He wills to give us." Prayer is the means by
the use of which we appropriate to ourselves and gain for others
the gift of God's love. This Church of ours is not lacking in activity for good, but what a woeful lack of prayer there is; and, as a
consequence, how thin is the life of the Church. The human element is magnified; the divine element is neglected. The Church
lacks power in the world because it fails in its work of prayer.
Prayer is intercourse with God, association with Him personally
and lovingly. We are eager enough to do His work, but we are
slow to go to Him for the power with which to work.

—Shirley Carter Hughson, OHC, *The Spiritual Letters of
Father Hughson* (1953)[28]

The idolatry of money means that the moral worth of a person is
judged in terms of the amount of money possessed or controlled.
The acquisition and accumulation of money in itself is considered
evidence of virtue. . . . Where money is an idol, to be poor is a sin.
This is an obscene idea of justification, directly in contradiction
with the Bible. In the gospel none are saved by any works of their
own, least of all by the mere acquisition of money. . . . The notion
of justification by acquisition of money is empirically absurd, for
it oversimplifies the relationship of the prosperous and the poor
and overlooks the dependence of the rich upon the poor for their
wealth. In this world human beings live at each other's expense,
and the affluence of the few is proximately related to, and supported by, the poverty of the many.

—William Stringfellow, "Money," in *A Keeper of the Word:
Selected Writings of William Stringfellow*[29]

The mark of God's church is fragmentation, the eucharistic mark
of brokenness. We are the body of Christ, and our ministry ought
to look like him. For the sake of unity and for the making of a
new humanity, this body—the church—may find its ministry in a
rending that forever breaks down walls and rips the Temple veil.

The unity God seeks and the new humanity God is making demand a place where all sorts and conditions can meet and be reconciled. To be that place, in this world, we shall have to be broken. We shall have to be torn from the idols of our own ideals. Our orthodoxy will be ruined, and our purity will be sullied. The stones of our walls of division, the rocks with which we have routed the sinner from our midst, will be reduced to sand. The banquets we have made of our resources and by which we have fed ourselves to fatness will be reduced to crumbs. And not to decide may be the hardest decision of all. The good news, then, may be that those energies we have given for so long to the vain dream of building sanctuaries of sameness may now be given to meeting one another in all our myriad differentness.

—Sam Portaro, *Conflict and a Christian Life* (1996)[30]

QUESTIONS FOR REFLECTION AND DISCUSSION

1. This chapter begins with the experience of Frances Perkins at the scene of a tragic fire that propelled her into a life of advocating for the safety of workers. Can you recall a moment of great insight or trauma that compelled you to act for the welfare of others? What continues to motivate you in your efforts to work for a more just society?

2. Many people see injustice in the world and yet are unable or unwilling to take concrete steps that would change the situation or make a difference. What most often keeps you from taking those steps? What hinders your attempts to act on what you believe and to "strive for justice and peace"?

3. In the passage immediately preceding these questions Sam Portaro challenges us to ministry in a church that is marked by fragmentation and brokenness, diversity and difference. Who challenges you the most when it comes to respecting the differences and dignity of other people? Why? How could you learn more about that person or group, in order to grow in understanding and respect?

Endnotes

Introduction

1. Norvene Vest, *Preferring Christ: A Devotional Commentary on the Rule of St. Benedict* (Harrisburg, Pa.: Morehouse Publishing, 2004), 16.

2. *Didache,* Roberts-Donaldson translation, *Early Christian Writings;* found at http://www.earlychristianwritings.com/didache.html.

3. Brian D. McLaren, *Finding Our Way Again: The Return of the Ancient Practices* (Nashville, Tenn.: Thomas Nelson, 2008), 3.

4. McLaren, *Finding Our Way Again,* 5.

5. Philip Sheldrake, *Spirituality and History,* new ed. (Maryknoll, N.Y.: Orbis Books,1995), 4.

6. Sheldrake, *Spirituality and History,* 86.

7. Phyllis Tickle, *The Great Emergence: How Christianity Is Changing and Why* (Grand Rapids, Mich.: Baker Books, 2008), 16–17, 51.

8. Vida Scudder, *Socialism and Character* (Boston: Houghton Mifflin, 1912), 346.

9. Tickle, *Great Emergence,* 141.

10. Esther de Waal, *Seeking Life: The Baptismal Invitation of the Rule of St. Benedict* (Collegeville, Minn.: Liturgical Press, 2009), 26.

11. Quoted in de Waal, *Seeking Life,* 26.

12. Sheldrake, *Spirituality and History,* 67.

13. de Waal, *Seeking Life,* 4.

Chapter 1

1. Cyprian, *To Donatus,* quoted in *Born to New Life: Cyprian of Carthage,* ed. and trans. Oliver Davies (New York: New City Press, 1992), 21–22.

2. John Gaden, "The Experience of the Easter Mystery," in *A Vision of Wholeness,* ed. Duncan Reid (Sydney: E. J. Dwyer, 1994), 281–82.

3. Byron David Stuhlman, *Occasions of Grace: An Historical and Theological Study of the Pastoral Offices and Episcopal Services in the Book of Common Prayer* (New York: Church Hymnal, 1995), 61.

4. Louis Weil, "Baptism as the Model for a Sacramental Aesthetic," *Anglican Theological Review* 92, no. 2 (Spring 2010): 261.

5. Paul Bradshaw, *Early Christian Worship: A Basic Introduction to Ideas and Practice* (Collegeville, Minn.: Liturgical Press, 1996), 2.

6. Cyril of Jerusalem, "Of Baptism," *On the Mysteries*, II.4.

7. Theodore of Mopsuestia, *Commentary of Theodore of Mopsuestia on the Lord's Prayer and on the Sacraments of Baptism and the Eucharist*, ed. A. Mingana (Cambridge: W. Heffer & Sons, 1933), 52–54.

8. Marion Hatchett, *Commentary on the American Book of Common Prayer* (New York: Seabury Press, 1980), 281.

9. John Chrysostom, *Baptismal Instructions*, II.27.

10. Weil, "Baptism," 261.

11. Augustine of Hippo, Sermon 57, "On the Holy Eucharist."

12. Daniel B. Stevick, *Baptismal Moments; Baptismal Meanings* (New York: Church Hymnal, 1987), 117.

13. Weil, "Baptism," 269–70.

14. Gregory of Tours, *History of the Franks*, Book II; found at http://www.fordham.edu/halsall/source/gregory-clovisconv.html.

15. Quoted in David Cressy, *Birth, Marriage and Death: Ritual, Religion, and the Life-Cycle in Tudor and Stuart England* (Oxford: Oxford University Press, 1997), 192.

16. Stevick, *Baptismal Moments*, 45, 118.

17. Stevick, *Baptismal Moments*, 119, 137–38, 158.

Chapter 2

1. From Sermon XIX, "Passion of Alban, Martyr," in *Aelfric's Lives of Saints: Being a Set of Sermons on Saints' Days formerly observed by the English Church*, ed. Walter Skeat (London: N. Trübner & Co., 1881), 415–19. Text lightly modernized.

2. Virginia Burrus and Rebecca Lyman, "Shifting the Focus of History," in *Late Ancient Christianity*, ed. Virginia Burrus, A People's History of Christianity, vol. 2 (Minneapolis, Minn.: Augsburg Fortress, 2005), 6.

3. Ignatius of Antioch, *Letter to the Trallians*, 6.

4. Rebecca Lyman, *Early Christian Traditions*, The New Church's Teaching Series, vol. 6 (Cambridge, Mass.: Cowley Publications, 1999), 38.

5. Irenaeus, *Against Heresies*, 4.33.8, as translated in Lyman, *Early Christian Traditions*, 57.

6. Irenaeus, *Against Heresies*, 3.15.2.

7. Harry O. Maier, "Heresy, Households, and the Disciplining of Diversity," *Late Ancient Christianity*, 227–29.

8. Tertullian, *Prescription against Heretics*, 41.

9. Martin L. Smith, *Compass and Stars* (New York: Seabury Books, 2007), 51–52.

10. *Apostolic Tradition* 21, quoted in Paul Bradshaw, *Early Christian Worship: A Basic Introduction to Ideas and Practice* (Collegeville, Minn.: Liturgical Press, 1996), 18–19.

11. Marianne H. Micks, *Loving the Questions: An Exploration of the Nicene Creed* (New York: Seabury Books, 2005), 10.

12. Lyman, *Early Christian Traditions,* 120.

13. Burrus and Lyman, "Shifting the Focus of History," 4.

14. Quoted in Tim Dowley, *Introduction to the History of Christianity* (Minneapolis, Minn.: Fortress Press, 2002), 176.

15. Athanasius, *Epistle against Epictetum*; Gregory of Nazianzus, *Epistle to Cledonius the Priest Against Apollinarius.*

16. Gordon MacDonald, *Ordering Your Private World* (Nashville, Tenn.: Thomas Nelson, 2003), 198.

17. *Didache* 9.

18. Justin, *I Apologia, 67*.3–7.

19. Andrew McGowan, in "Food, Ritual, and Power," in *Late Ancient Christianity,* 157.

20. Lyman, *Early Christian Traditions,* 3.

21. Richard Hooker, *The Laws of Ecclesiastical Polity,* IV.2.

22. Michael Ramsey, *The Gospel and the Catholic Church,* as quoted in *To Believe Is to Pray: Readings from Michael Ramsey,* ed. James E. Griffiss (Cambridge, Mass.: Cowley Publications, 1996), 150–51.

23. Brian D. McLaren, *Finding Our Way Again: The Return of the Ancient Practices* (Nashville, Tenn.: Thomas Nelson, 2008), 5.

24. Patrick Malloy, "Rick Warren Meets Gregory Dix: The Liturgical Movement Comes Knocking at the Megachurch Door," *Anglican Theological Review* 92, no. 3 (Summer 2010): 449.

25. Geoffrey Rowell, Kenneth Stevenson, and Rowan Williams, eds., *Love's Redeeming Work: The Anglican Quest for Holiness* (Oxford: Oxford University Press, 2001), xxvii–xxviii.

26. Rowell, Stevenson, and Williams, eds., *Love's Redeeming Work,* xxviii.

27. Robert Webber, *Ancient-Future Worship: Proclaiming and Enacting God's Narrative* (Grand Rapids, Mich.: Baker Academic, 2008), 162.

28. Mark McIntosh, *Mysteries of Faith,* The New Church's Teaching Series, vol. 8 (Cambridge, Mass.: Cowley Publications, 2000), 12.

29. Barbara Brown Taylor, "Way Beyond Belief: The Call to Behold," in *Shouts and Whispers: Twenty-One Writers Speak about Their Writing and Their Faith,* ed. Jennifer L. Holberg (Grand Rapids, Mich.: Eerdmans, 2006), 11.

Chapter 3

1. Richard Rolle, Prologue to the Psalter, in *Richard Rolle: The English Writings*, trans. and ed. Rosamund S. Allen (Mahwah, N.J.: Paulist Press, 1988), 66–67.

2. Barbara Brown Taylor, *Speaking of Sin* (Cambridge, Mass.: Cowley Publications, 2000), 28.

3. Geoffrey Rowell, Kenneth Stevenson, and Rowan Williams, eds., *Love's Redeeming Work: The Anglican Quest for Holiness* (Oxford: Oxford University Press, 2001), xxvii.

4. Esther de Waal, *Seeking Life: The Baptismal Invitation of the Rule of St. Benedict* (Collegeville, Minn.: Liturgical Press, 2009), 96.

5. Byron David Stuhlman, *The Initiatory Process in the Byzantine Tradition,* Gorgias Eastern Christian Studies 18 (Piscataway, N.J.: Gorgias Press, 2009), 77.

6. Theodore of Mopsuestia, *Commentary on the Lord's Prayer, Baptism and the Eucharist*, chapter 3.

7. *The Rule of St. Benedict,* chapter 72.

8. Joan Chittister, OSB, *The Rule of Benedict: Insights for the Ages* (New York: Crossroad, 1992), 178.

9. Esther de Waal, *Every Earthly Blessing: Rediscovering the Celtic Tradition* (Harrisburg, Pa.: Morehouse Publishing, 1999), 14–15.

10. Margaret Guenther, *At Home in the World: A Rule of Life for the Rest of Us* (New York: Seabury Books, 2006), 11, 13.

11. See, for example, Margaret Guenther, *The Art of Spiritual Direction* (Cambridge, Mass.: Cowley Publications, 1992); Norvene Vest, ed., *Still Listening: New Horizons in Spiritual Direction* (Harrisburg, Pa.: Morehouse Publishing, 2000); and Alan Jones, *Exploring Spiritual Direction* (Cambridge, Mass.: Cowley Publications, 1999).

12. Phyllis Tickle, *The Divine Hours: Prayers for Summertime* (New York: Doubleday, 2000), viii.

13. Tickle, *Divine Hours: Summertime* (New York: Doubleday, 2000), ix.

14. Simon Jones, *"Opus Dei,"* in *The Oblate Life,* ed. Gervase Holdaway, OSB (Collegeville, Minn.: Liturgical Press, 2008), 81–82.

15. Diana Butler Bass, *A People's History of Christianity: The Other Side of the Story* (New York: HarperOne, 2009), 107–08.

16. Tickle, *Divine Hours: Summertime,* x–xi.

17. Rowell, Stevenson, and Williams, *Love's Redeeming Work,* 5.

18. Edwin Sandys, "The Fourth Sermon ('I exhort therefore')," in *The Sermons of Edwin Sandys,* ed. J. Ayre (Cambridge: Parker Society, 1842), 76–77.

19. William Perkins, "A Graine of Mustard-Seede," in *The Works of William Perkins,* ed. J. Breward (Appleford, Berks.: Sutton Courtenay Press, 1970), 409.

20. Thomas Becon, *The Pathway Unto Prayer,* in *The Early Works of Thomas Becon,* ed. John Ayre (Cambridge: Parker Society, 1843), 170–71.

21. Jeremy Taylor, *Holy Living,* ed. Hal M. Helms (Orleans, Mass.: Paraclete Press, 1988), 3–4, 8–9, 11–12, 16, 20, 28.

22. Thomas Traherne, *Centuries* (London: Mowbray, 1985), 13–14.

23. Father John-Julian OJN, ed. and trans., *A Lesson of Love: The Revelations of Julian of Norwich* (New York: Walker and Company, 1988), 11–13.

24. Esther de Waal, *The Celtic Way of Prayer: The Recovery of the Religious Imagination* (New York: Image Books, 1997), x.

25. Nancy Roth, *Organic Prayer* (New York: Seabury Books, 2007), 5–7.

26. Rowell, Stevenson, and Williams, eds., *Love's Redeeming Work,* xix–xx.

27. Charles Williams, ed., *The Letters of Evelyn Underhill* (Westminster, Md.: Christian Classics, 1989), 71–72.

28. Esther de Waal, *A Life-Giving Way: A Commentary on the Rule of St. Benedict* (Collegeville, Minn.: Liturgical Press, 1995), ix–x.

29. Katharine Jefferts Schori, *A Wing and a Prayer* (Harrisburg, Pa.: Morehouse Publishing, 2007), 100–101.

Chapter 4

1. From "The Four Kamehamehas" in *Mission Life,* Vol. VI (March 1, 1869); 135–42; found at http://anglicanhistory.org/hawaii/kamehamehas1869.html.

2. O. C. Edwards, Jr., *A History of Preaching,* vol. 1 (Nashville, Tenn.: Abingdon Press, 2004), 3.

3. George Herbert, *The Country Parson,* in *George Herbert: The Country Parson and the Temple,* ed. John Nelson Wall (Mahwah, N.J.: Paulist Press, 1981), 62–63.

4. John Donne, from "Now in a Glass, Then Face to Face," a sermon preached at St. Paul's Cathedral for Easter Day (1628), in *John Donne: Selections from* Divine Poems, Sermons, Devotions, *and Prayers,* ed. John Booty (Mahwah, N.J.: Paulist Press, 1990), 143–44.

5. From the Prologue to the translation of the Bible by Miles Coverdale (1535); found at http://www.archive.org/stream/writingstranslat00cove/writingstranslat00cove_djvu.txt.

6. Quoted in F. F. Bruce, *History of the Bible in English* (Cambridge: Lutterworth Press, 1979), 68.

7. Diarmaid MacCulloch, *Christianity: The First Three Thousand Years* (New York: Viking, 2009), 581–82.

8. Jeremy Taylor, "The Diary: Or, Rule to spend each Day religiously," in *The Golden Grove, or, A Manuall of Daily Prayers and Letanies* (London: R. Royston, 1655); found at http://anglicanhistory.org/taylor/golden/diary.html.

9. Jean Leclercq, OSB, *The Love of Learning and the Desire for God: A Study of Monastic Culture* (New York: Fordham University Press, 1982), 16, 73.

10. Taylor, "The Diary."

11. Richard Kieckheffer, "Major Currents in Late Medieval Devotion," in *Christian Spirituality: High Middle Ages and Reformation*, ed. Jill Raitt, World Spirituality: An Encyclopedic History of the Religious Quest, vol. 17 (New York: Crossroad, 1996), 77.

12. Edwards, *History of Preaching*, 210–11.

13. Edwards, *History of Preaching*, 474–75.

14. Edwards, *History of Preaching*, 378.

15. Phillips Brooks, *Lectures on Preaching, delivered before the Divinity School of Yale College in January and February, 1877* (New York: E. P. Dutton and Co., 1877), 21.

16. Barbara Brown Taylor, *The Preaching Life* (Cambridge, Mass.: Cowley Publications, 1993), 48–49, 90.

17. From the recollections of Thomas Fuller, quoted in Edwards, *History of Preaching*, 369.

18. Taylor, *Preaching Life*, 47.

19. Augustine, *The Uses of Rhetoric*, quoted in Richard Lischer, ed., *The Company of Preachers: Wisdom on Preaching, Augustine to the Present* (Grand Rapids, Mich.: Eerdmans, 2002), 283.

20. Richard Baxter, *The Reformed Pastor*, quoted in Lischer, *Company of Preachers*, 74.

21. Gregory the Great, *Pastoral Rule*, quoted in Lischer, *Company of Preachers*, 356.

22. Taylor, *Preaching Life*, 47.

23. Eamon Duffy, *Marking the Hours: English People and Their Prayers, 1240–1570* (New Haven, Conn.: Yale University Press, 2006), 25.

24. Duffy, *Marking the Hours*, 114, 104.

25. Bede, *The Ecclesiastical History of the English Nation* (New York: E. P. Dutton, 1910), preface to Book I.

26. Leclercq, *Love of Learning*, 166.

27. From the preface to *Holy Women, Holy Men* (New York: Church Publishing, 2010), x.

28. Leclercq, *Love of Learning*, 176.

29. Charles Williams, ed., *The Letters of Evelyn Underhill* (Westminster, Md.: Christian Classics, 1989), 313.

30. Williams, *Letters of Evelyn Underhill*, 66.

31. Williams, *Letters of Evelyn Underhill*, 224–25.

32. Williams, *Letters of Evelyn Underhill*, 312–13.

33. Williams, *Letters of Evelyn Underhill*, 189–90.

34. Ruthanna B. Hooke, *Transforming Preaching* (New York: Church Publishing, 2010), 28.

Chapter 5

1. From an Easter letter of Dionysius, quoted in Eusebius, *Ecclesiastical History,* 7.22.

2. *The Sisters of St. Mary at Memphis: with the Acts and Sufferings of the Priests and Others Who Were There with Them during the Yellow Fever Season of 1878* (New York: Printed, but not Published, 1879); found at http://anglicanhistory.org/usa/csm/memphis1.html.

3. Tertullian, *Apology,* 39, quoted in Diana Butler Bass, *A People's History of Christianity: The Other Side of the Story* (New York: HarperOne, 2009), 64–65.

4. Bass, *A People's History,* 64.

5. Esther de Waal, *Seeking God: The Way of St. Benedict* (Collegeville, Minn.: Liturgical Press, 1984), 120.

6. *The Rule of the Society of Saint John the Evangelist* (Cambridge, Mass.: Cowley Publications, 1997), 69.

7. de Waal, *Seeking God,* 121.

8. Bass, *A People's History,* 95.

9. From an account by Goscelin of Saint-Bertin, quoted in John Blair, *The Church in Anglo-Saxon Society* (Oxford: Oxford University Press, 2005), 368.

10. Blair, *The Church in Anglo-Saxon Society,* 506.

11. Prologue, *The Rule of St. Benedict,* trans. Luke Dysinger, OSB, quoted in Norvene Vest, *Preferring Christ: A Devotional Commentary on the Rule of St. Benedict* (Harrisburg, Pa.: Morehouse Publishing, 2004).

12. Esther de Waal, *Living with Contradiction: Reflections on the Rule of St. Benedict* (San Francisco: Harper & Row, 1989), 69.

13. Rowan Williams, "God's Workshop," an address at "Shaping Holy Lives: A Conference on Benedictine Spirituality," Trinity Church, New York, 2003; found at http://www.archbishopofcanterbury.org/1698.

14. David Knowles, *The Monastic Order in England* (Cambridge: Cambridge University Press, 1963), 24.

15. Bede, *A History of the English Church and People,* trans. Leo Sherley-Price (New York: Penguin Books, 1968), 248.

16. Bede, *History of the English Church,* 247.

17. Francis Turner and T. M. Macdonogh, *Brief Memoirs of Nicholas Ferrar* (London: James Nisbet, 1837), 120–21.

18. Turner and Macdonogh, *Brief Memoirs,* 123

19. *The Rule of the Society of Saint John the Evangelist,* 86–87.

20. Cyprian of Carthage, *On the Unity of the Church,* found at http://www.ccel.org/ccel/schaff/anf05.iv.v.i.html.

21. Joan Chittister, *The Rule of Benedict: Insights for the Ages* (New York: Crossroad, 1996), 177.

22. C. S. Lewis, "Answers to Questions on Christianity," in *God in the Dock: Essays on Theology and Ethics* (Grand Rapids, Mich.: Eerdmans, 1970), 61–62.

23. Verna J. Dozier, *Confronted By God: The Essential Verna Dozier,* ed. Cynthia L. Shattuck and Fredrica Harris Thompsett (New York: Seabury Books, 2006), 44.

24. Suzanne Guthrie, *Praying the Hours* (Cambridge, Mass.: Cowley Publications, 2000), 61–64.

25. Michael Battle, "A Strange Route to Heaven," in *Heaven* ed. Roger Ferlo (New York: Seabury Books, 2007), 155.

Chapter 6

1. Frances Perkins, "Not in Vain," in Leon Stein, *Out of the Sweatshop: The Struggle for Industrial Democracy* (New York: Quadrangle, 1977), 200.

2. Quoted in Leon Stein and William Greider, *The Triangle Fire* (New York: Cornell University Press, 2001), x.

3. Perkins, "Not in Vain," 201.

4. Harold T. Lewis, *Christian Social Witness,* The New Church's Teaching Series, vol. 10 (Cambridge, Mass.: Cowley Publications, 2001), 1.

5. Marianne H. Micks, *Loving the Questions: An Exploration of the Nicene Creed* (New York: Seabury Books, 2005), 103.

6. C. René Padilla, "God's Call to Do Justice," in *The Justice Project,* ed. Brian McLaren, Elisa Padilla, and Ashley Bunting Seeber, (Grand Rapids, Mich.: Baker Books, 2009), 25.

7. James E. Griffiss, *The Anglican Vision,* The New Church's Teaching Series, vol. 1 (Cambridge, Mass.: Cowley Publications, 1997), 51.

8. Bede, *A History of the English Church and People,* trans. Leo Sherley Price (New York: Penguin Books, 1968), II.1.

9. John Thrupp, *The Anglo-Saxon Home: A History of the Domestic Institutions and Customs of England, From the Fifth to the Eleventh Century* (London: Longman, Green, Longman, & Roberts, 1862), 135.

10. Frederick Douglass, *The Life and Times of Frederick Douglass: His Early Life as a Slave, His Escape from Bondage, and His Complete History, Written by Himself* (Cleveland: Ohio: Hamilton, Rewell, & Co., 1883), 73–74.

11. Quoted in G. Scott Cady and Christopher L. Webber, *A Year With American Saints* (New York: Church Publishing, 2006), 337.

12. Christopher Hall, "A 'Letter to Florence' on the Diamond Jubilee of her Priesting"; found at http://www.litim-oi.org/letter-2.html.

13. Pamela W. Darling, *New Wine: The Story of Women Transforming Leadership and Power in the Episcopal Church* (Cambridge, Mass.: Cowley Publications, 1994), 180.

14. From a statement made to the House of Bishops by Bishop Paul Jones on October 18, 1917, quoted in Don S. Armentrout and Robert Boak Slocum, eds., *Documents of Witness: A History of the Episcopal Church 1782–1985* (New York: Church Publishing, 1984), 339–40.

15. From the Episcopal Peace Fellowship website: http://epfnational.org/.

16. Quoted in John Howard Melish, *Bishop Paul Jones: Witness for Peace* (Cincinnati, Ohio: Forward Movement Publications, 1992), 54.

17. Rowan Williams, "Theology and Economics: Two Different Worlds?" *Anglican Theological Review* 92, no. 4 (Fall 2010): 611.

18. William Tyndale, "The Parable of the Wicked Mammon," in *Doctrinal Treatises . . . by William Tyndale,* ed. Henry Walter (Cambridge: Parker Society, 1848), 93. Text lightly modernized.

19. F. D. Maurice, *The Kingdom of Christ*; quoted in Lewis, *Christian Social Witness,* 31.

20. Vida Dutton Scudder, *On Journey* (New York: E. P. Dutton, 1937), 72.

21. Emily Malbone Morgan, *Letters to Her Companions,* ed. Vida Dutton Scudder (South Byfield, Mass.: SCHC, 1944), 120.

22. Joanna B. Gillespie: "The Companions of the Holy Cross: A Vocation to Prayer Companionship," in *Deeper Joy: Lay Women and Vocation in the 20th Century Episcopal Church,* ed. Fredrica Harris Thompsett and Sheryl Kujawa-Holbrook, (New York: Church Publishing, 2005), 62.

23. Quoted in Jacqueline Schmitt, "'Sacrificial Adventure': Episcopal Women of the Progressive Era," in Thompsett and Kujawa-Holbrook, *Deeper Joy,* 191.

24. Printed in the *Boston Transcript* (1912), quoted in Schmitt, "'Sacrificial Adventure,'" 189.

25. Anglican Communion Office, *The Virginia Report* 2.20, 2.26.

26. John S. Mogabgab, "Editor's Introduction," *Weavings* 24, no. 2 (March/April 2009): 3.

27. William Temple radio broadcast of August 1939, quoted in F. A. Iremonger, *William Temple, Archbishop of Canterbury: His Life and Letters* (London: Oxford University Press, 1948), 540.

28. Shirley Carter Hughson, OHC, *The Spiritual Letters of Father Hughson* (London: Mowbray, 1953), 64–65.

29. William Stringfellow, *A Keeper of the Word: Selected Writings of William Stringfellow,* ed. Bill Wylie Kellermann (Grand Rapids, Mich.: Eerdmans, 1994), 245–46.

30. Sam Portaro, *Conflict and a Christian Life* (Harrisburg, Pa.: Morehouse Publishing, 1996), 98–99.

Suggestions for Further Reading

Backhouse, Robert, comp. *A Feast of Anglican Spirituality.* London: Canterbury Press Norwich, 1998.

Bass, Diana Butler. *A People's History of Christianity: The Other Side of the Story.* New York: HarperOne, 2009.

Black, Vicki K., comp. *Speaking to the Soul: Daily Readings for the Christian Year.* Harrisburg, Pa.: Morehouse Publishing, 2009.

Duffy, Eamon. *Marking the Hours: English People and Their Prayers, 1240–1570.* New Haven, Conn.: Yale University Press, 2006.

Edwards, O. C., Jr. *A History of Preaching.* 2 vols. Nashville, Tenn.: Abingdon Press, 2004.

Guenther, Margaret. *The Art of Spiritual Direction.* Cambridge, Mass.: Cowley Publications, 1992.

———. *At Home in the World: A Rule of Life for the Rest of Us.* New York: Seabury Books, 2006.

Holdaway, Gervase, OSB, ed. *The Oblate Life.* Collegeville, Minn.: Liturgical Press, 2008.

Holy Women, Holy Men. New York: Church Publishing, 2010.

Hooke, Ruthanna B. *Transforming Preaching.* New York: Church Publishing, 2010.

John-Julian, OJN. *Stars in a Dark World: Stories of the Saints and Holy Days of the Liturgy.* Denver, Colo.: Outskirts Press, 2009.

Jones, Alan, *Exploring Spiritual Direction.* Cambridge, Mass.: Cowley Publications, 1999.

Jones, Cheslyn, Geoffrey Wainwright, and Edward Yarnold, SJ, eds. *The Study of Liturgy.* New York: Oxford University Press, 1978.

Leclercq, Jean, OSB. *The Love of Learning and the Desire for God: A Study of Monastic Culture.* New York: Fordham University Press, 1982.

Lewis, Harold T. *Christian Social Witness,* The New Church's Teaching Series, vol. 10. Cambridge, Mass.: Cowley Publications, 2001.

Lischer, Richard, ed. *The Company of Preachers: Wisdom on Preaching, Augustine to the Present.* Grand Rapids, Mich.: Eerdmans, 2002.

Lyman, Rebecca. *Early Christian Traditions,* The New Church's Teaching Series, vol. 6. Cambridge, Mass.: Cowley Publications, 1999.

MacCulloch, Diarmaid. *Christianity: The First Three Thousand Years.* New York: Viking, 2009.

McIntosh, Mark. *Mysteries of Faith,* The New Church's Teaching Series, vol. 8. Cambridge, Mass.: Cowley Publications, 2000.

McLaren, Brian D. *Finding Our Way Again: The Return of the Ancient Practices.* Nashville, Tenn.: Thomas Nelson, 2008.

McQuiston, John. *Always We Begin Again: The Benedictine Way of Living.* Harrisburg, Pa.: Morehouse Publishing, 1996.

Meyers, Ruth A. *Continuing the Reformation: Re-Visioning Baptism in the Episcopal Church.* New York: Church Publishing, 1997.

Micks, Marianne H. *Deep Waters: An Introduction to Baptism.* Cambridge, Mass.: Cowley Publications, 1996.

———. H. *Loving the Questions: An Exploration of the Nicene Creed.* New York: Seabury Books, 2005.

Rowell, Geoffrey, Kenneth Stevenson, and Rowan Williams, eds. *Love's Redeeming Work: The Anglican Quest for Holiness.* Oxford: Oxford University Press, 2001.

The Rule of the Society of Saint John the Evangelist. Cambridge, Mass.: Cowley Publications, 1997.

Sheldrake, Philip. *Spirituality and History.* Maryknoll, N.Y.: Orbis Books, 1995.

Spinks, Bryan D. *Early and Medieval Rituals and Theologies of Baptism: From the New Testament to the Council of Trent.* Aldershot, UK: Ashgate Publishing, 2006.

———. *Reformation and Modern Rituals and Theologies of Baptism: From Luther to Contemporary Practices.* Aldershot, UK: Ashgate Publishing, 2006.

Stevick, Daniel B. *Baptismal Moments; Baptismal Meanings.* New York: Church Hymnal, 1987.

Taylor, Barbara Brown. *Speaking of Sin.* Cambridge, Mass.: Cowley Publications, 2000.

Thompsett, Fredrica Harris. *Living with History,* The New Church's Teaching Series, vol. 5. Cambridge, Mass.: Cowley Publications, 1999.

Thompsett, Fredrica Harris, and Sheryl Kujawa-Holbrook, eds. *Deeper Joy: Lay Women and Vocation in the 20th Century Episcopal Church.* New York: Church Publishing, 2005.

Tickle, Phyllis. *The Divine Hours: Prayers for Summertime.* New York: Doubleday, 2000.

———. *The Great Emergence: How Christianity Is Changing and Why.* Grand Rapids, Mich.: Baker Books, 2008.

Vest, Norvene. *Preferring Christ: A Devotional Commentary on the Rule of St. Benedict.* Harrisburg, Pa.: Morehouse Publishing, 2004.

———. ed. *Still Listening: New Horizons in Spiritual Direction.* Harrisburg, Pa.: Morehouse Publishing, 2000.

de Waal, Esther. *Every Earthly Blessing: Rediscovering the Celtic Tradition.* Harrisburg, Pa.: Morehouse Publishing, 1999.

———. *A Life-Giving Way: A Commentary on the Rule of St. Benedict.* Collegeville, Minn.: Liturgical Press, 1995.

———. *Seeking Life: The Baptismal Invitation of the Rule of St. Benedict.* Collegeville, Minn.: Liturgical Press, 2009.

Ward, Benedicta. *High King of Heaven: Aspects of Early English Spirituality.* London: Mowbray, 1999.

Westerhoff, Caroline. *Calling: A Song for the Baptized.* New York: Seabury Classics, 1994, 2005.

Wolf, William J., ed. *The Spirit of Anglicanism.* London: T & T Clark, 1982.

www.ingramcontent.com/pod-product-compliance
Lightning Source LLC
Jackson TN
JSHW081317130125
77033JS00011B/321